The Destroyers

American University Studies

Series XI
Anthropology and Sociology

Vol. 17

PETER LANG
New York · Bern · Frankfurt am Main · Paris

James Kern Feibleman

The Destroyers

The Underside of Human Nature

PETER LANG
New York · Bern · Frankfurt am Main · Paris

Library of Congress Cataloging-in-Publication Data

Feibleman, James Kern
  The destroyers.

  (American university studies. Series XI,
Anthropology and sociology ; vol. 17)
  Includes index.
  1. Violence.   2. Aggressiveness (Psychology)
3. Murder.   4. Human behavior.   I. Title.   II. Series:
American university studies. Series XI, Anthropology/
sociology ; vol. 17.
HM291.F38   1987   303.6'2   87-3548
ISBN 0-8204-0609-0
ISSN 0740-0497

CIP-Kurztitelaufnahme der Deutschen Bibliothek

Feibleman, James Kern:
The destroyers : the underside of human nature /
James Kern Feibleman. — New York; Bern;
Frankfurt am Main; Paris: Lang 1987
  (American University Studies: Ser. 11,
  Anthropology and Sociology; Vol. 17)
  ISBN 0-8204-0609-0

NE: American University Studies / 11

© Peter Lang Publishing, Inc., New York 1987

Printed by Weihert-Druck GmbH, Darmstadt, West Germany

TABLE OF

CONTENTS

PREFACE

The last few decades have impressed me with the prevalence all over the world not of love but of hate, not of help but of hurt, not of tolerance but of murder; and I came to realize that humanity would not benefit from the refusal to recognize how widespread was aggression. Of course there will always be a modicum of animosity in human affairs, and even some overt hostility; but it has never been as virulent as now. In the degree to which it has come to prevail in recent national and international affairs, it can be regarded only as a social ailment, and one which may possibly be fatal.

Applied biologists have always had to confront the problem of disease: its cure and prevention; and they have met with some notable successes: tuberculosis has been conquered and polio eradicated. Cancer now engages much of their attention.

I think that aggression must be regarded in much the same fashion: studied in order to discover its causes, with a view to finding an antidote. We must learn how to neutralize this poison before it does away with us. I intend here to contribute to that effort by examining the many forms of aggression and if possible by locating its core. That should make the task easier for the next investigator to look for a method of eliminating it altogether.

I should note that throughout this book I use the term 'man' as short-hand for 'humankind', not as a name for a particular sex. I find this usage more convenient than the awkward 'man or woman', 'he or she'. I mean therefore no derogation of the female sex, which I have always assumed, even before the feminist movement, to be the equal in all respects of the male.

I want to thank my very able assistant, Mrs. Clair Wessing, for her generous help in preparing the typescript.

New Orleans, Louisiana
February, 1987

Chapter 1

THE BACKGROUND

Why is there so much aggressive behavior on the part of human beings? That is not an easy question because aggression takes so many forms, but any answer would have to take into consideration the fact that there is one and only one human species. Perhaps what any of its members do, others could have done given the proper circumstances.

The last statement may be difficult to accept, yet all the evidence is in its favor. The thesis that man is always ready to be a killer must be completely obvious to anyone who has impartially examined the facts. It would seem that we are individually capable of all kinds of reprehensive behavior if the occasion should call them out in us.[1] More than that: only too often we do nothing to stop the worst offences.

The first step to take in the effort to solve a problem is to learn that you have one. We face currently an increasing use of violence to settle social problems. It is perhaps foolish to expect us to find a solution when we ourselves are part of the problem, idle to place any faith in human nature when it is human nature that is responsible. The widespread killing of human beings by other human beings, so prevalent a practice nowadays, is after all the work of human beings; and if we seek to understand the terrible times of destruction in which we happen to live, then we must look for its causes deep in the past, with its ancient roots in pre-human epochs. Since the task of sociology is to study all repeating patterns of behavior, it would be an error to leave out wars, torture, terrorism, murders, cannibalism, massacres, and the like, or the absolute beliefs which so often provide their motivation.

Has there ever been an animal species so full of variety as the human? The enormous range of choices of action has seldom been explored on its own, yet this needs doing if we wish to understand history as well as to organize our thoughts in order to influence the future.

On the basis of any chosen criterion we can see a bewildering set of alternatives that run right through the entire spectrum. For instances, some individuals wish to amass all the wealth in the world while others give all they have to the poor. Some in every sample of the population are psychopaths while others are altruists; some are killers for the sheer pleasure of killing while others sacrifice their lives to save the lives of total strangers; some wish to build what they can to benefit future gener- ations while others only want to knock down what has been constructed in the past.

Every generation probably contains members of all these groups but in unequal proportions. What bring out the differences in actions probably depends upon many factors: social events, developments in knowledge, probably even lack of memory. These are the elements which cannot be properly analyzed until we have learned how to assess the effects of material gains and losses, the impact of new ideas and the revival of old ones which have been neglected.

Despite everything that has happened, the belief persists somehow that all that we do lies within our control. We are the masters of our fate, or so we are convinced, and if we have been victimized by disasters of human provenience, why that situation can be easily changed by an act of will. "The key assumption that crumbles in a disaster", according to

R. Janoff-Bulman, a psychologist at the University of Massachusetts, "is that
of invulnerability, the sense that the world is benevolent, controllable and
fair, and that so long as one acts as one should, nothing untoward will
happen".[2] He was speaking of course of natural disasters, such as earth-
quakes and mud slides, but it might also be true of man-made disasters, such
as wars. In these cases we are our own victims, and no more able to control
human nature than any other nature.

There seems to be a rhythm to the life-cycles of cultures, but no one
has yet discovered what it is sufficiently to be able to make predictions.
Some periods in history are much more stable than others while some are more
violent. It is the latter which have been described by Russian historians
as "a time of troubles".[3]

Despite these episodes most of the writing about history has been favorable. Its prevailing tone is upbeat, with the emphasis on successes, on
organizations and constructions, which are taken as cumulative. When there
are interruptions, as for instance by social revolutions, these are usually
regarded as only temporary obstacles in he forward march of civilization.

This is certainly the view from the top side of the human spectacle, but
there is also the under side, which shows the vast and repeated struggles
of men against each other. In the following pages we shall be embarked on
the trail of the Furies as they follow man, the hunter and killer.

> From the union between Air and Mother Earth
> there sprang Terror, Anger, Strife, Lies,
> Oaths, Vengeance, Intemperance, Altercation,
> Treaty, Oblivion, Fear, Pride, Battle, and
> the three Erinnyes, or Furies, the avengers
> of crime. 4

"Peace is the dream of the wise", Richard Burton wrote, quoting an ancient
Oriental proverb, "war is the history of man".

The aim of this study, then, is to serve as a reminder of the kind of human nature which has been neglected by the writers of treatises in the humanist tradition. The endless variety of behavior never ceases to amaze those who observe it. Every possible custom, every conceivable institution within the reach of human capabilities, has been established in some culture, ancient or modern. For instance, everything that can be eaten has been eaten —— or prohibited for religious reasons —— somewhere and at some time. And the range of such behavior must include all of the destructive as well as constructive impulses and forces. Occasionally, of course there are peaceful efforts toward cooperation, but they are few and far between, and the majority movement has been the other way.

I have included enough data in each of the following chapters to make the point that I am not talking about exceptions to human behavior but rather about typical performances. A more exhaustive collection could easily be assembled given the modern computer and contemporary methods of information retrieval; if this were done, the evidence of destructive behavior described here would be overwhelming, for it is clearly on the increase.

Perhaps it is the price humanity has to pay for its unification. Certainly we will have to admit that the example of ancient Rome proves that a culture built on ruthless destructive methods of pacification is capable of furnishing the foundations for an orderly and lawful society. The only questions that remain are whether it is the only way one can be established and whether it is an inevitable result. In 146 BC the most civilized of the citizens of Athens were carried off to be the household slaves of wealthy Romans. It would not have been any satisfaction to them in their slavery to have known that in little more than a century Greek culture would have conquered its conquerors and the work of the

Greeks and their ancestors emulated in Roman society.

The establishment of the Roman Empire may have been an exception to the usual results of such brutal conquests, for most have had no constructive effects at all. It is not the preferred way to achieve stable and cultivated civilizations, which more often have had to survive wars rather than build on them. How awful to conclude that men turn to peaceful pursuits, such as the arts and sciences, and the practices of altruism, only when they have grown tired of fighting!

The sacred writings of the prophets who were founders of 'world' religions, from Moses to Mohammed, have proclaimed that man had to be redeemed in some way; which would indicate that they thought him essentially bad. It is a curious fact that this judgment, despite its widespread promulgation and acceptance, was reversed in recent times. Three separate developments were responsible for the change, especially in Europe and America: the writings of Rousseau, the discovery of Tahiti, and Darwin's theory of evolution.

Toward the end of the eighteenth century in Europe, the idea somehow took hold that man is essentially good and that it is government which makes him bad. If Jean-Jacques Rousseau did not originate this concept, at least his writings and teachings were at the center of it, for he thought that if only mankind could return to a state of nature, then all wars could be abolished and all conflicts and restrictions eliminated. In three discourses, the first published in 1750 and the last in 1762, Rousseau drew a picture of the "Noble Savage" as man in his earliest stages who was essentially good; one who had no instinct beyond survival and reproduction, his needs only for food, sleep and sex, with no ideas about property and hence no ambition or vice.

At about that time, the Frenchman Louis de Bougainville and the

Englishman James Cook discovered Tahiti and brought home idyllic reports that supported Rousseau's ideas. The natives there led ideal lives, making love, eating the fish and breadfruit that were so abundant, singing and dancing, and having evidently no other needs. War was unknown and everything material was held in common. Here, then, was a complete illustration of what Rousseau had been talking about, so that far from a visionary ideal, it evidently was an attainable reality. Tahiti was probably occupied for the first time about the ninth century of our era, though we do not know for certain, but there may have been such an isolation lasting a thousand years. In any case it was the most idyllic culture ever discovered before the arrival of westerners.

Early in the nineteenth century Charles Darwin, published his ideas of organic evolution in The Origin of Species, which introduced the idea of natural selection and seemed to suggest that just as man had developed from the ape, so with chance variations he could continue to improve. Even if this was not exactly what Darwin meant, it was what his ideas were taken to imply.

The optimistic view of human culture, then, was a result of the ideas of Rousseau and Darwin and the discovery of Tahiti, and it was going to be difficult to shake. It was a hardy view because it was what men of good will everywhere wanted to believe, and what they continued to believe to some extent even after two world wars.

The aggressive side of human nature has been in almost full command of much of the globe in recent decades. Most people already know about those two great wars, but not about the more frightening activity of human aggression in the time between wars when countless millions were the victims of torture and murder. From the peaceful intentions expressed in the 18th and 19th centuries to the massacres in the 20th represents an

enormous moral distance, but it is one which has been traversed by the
peoples of our own generations. It is in the main the story related in
this book.

Nobody has dared to tell people what they are really like, but maybe it
is time to do so and not leave them with an image of themselves which in the
end can be so harmful. Do they really know what they are doing? After all
the killing is over, if it ever is, given the destruction power of nuclear
weapons, those who are left behind may barely resemble human beings as we
have come to know them.

Evidently, the capacity for savage and unlimited aggression is never far
beneath the surface and stands ready to burst out at any moment on the
slightest provocation. The present study of destruction can never be an
entire world-view because the cosmos is more enduring. It is only on the
surface of the earth that everything can be destroyed, and whatever man
can do he probably will do.

The last hope is that if we really understood all of our native
tendencies, we could change those that are the most self-destructive. If
we truly grasped the fact that mankind is a single interbreeding species
but one so divided by absolute beliefs that the unity is forgotten, a
species more separated by little differences than brought together by
large similarities; and therefore if we recognized that in annihilating
others —— neighbors and enemies alike —— we are destroying ourselves;
knowing that in the end might save us.

Notes

1 Cf. e.g. J. D. Carthy and F. J. Ebling, The Natural History of
Aggression (London 1964, Academic Press), pp. 65-71; also
C. D. Clemente and D. B. Lindsley, Aggression and Defence (Berkeley
1967, University of California Press), passim.
2 Quoted in The New York Times from Daniel Goleman,
November 26, 1985, p. 17.

3 The most convenient reference is in A. J. Toynbee, <u>A Study of History</u> (Oxford 1934, University Press), vol. I, p. 53 n.2

4 Hesiod, <u>Theogony</u>, 211-232.

Chapter 2

THE HUNTERS

It is generally agreed that much of animal behavior can be accounted for
in terms of the effort to reduce the pressure of basic tissue-needs. Human
individuals, whatever else they may be, are animals, and they share the
needs of animals. Among the more exigent of the animal needs are those for
food, water and a mate; hunger, thirst and sexual desire being recognized as
the driving forces. Human behavior can be explained in the same way,
though to account for all of it requires suitable extensions.

Water has usually been easy enough to come by, it is to be found in
every stream and river, every pond and gully; but obtaining food called on
a more strenuous effort. Early man was a hunter and he remained one for
hundreds of thousands of years. This kind of past must have laid down deep
patterns of behavior which were hard to break. Indeed it can be argued that
they have not been broken.

According to Professor Burkert

> Man can virtually be defined as "the hunting
> ape"...[for] the age of the hunter, the
> Palaeolithic, comprises by far the largest
> part of human history....By comparison, the
> period since the invention of agriculture ——
> 10,000 years at most —— is a drop in the
> bucket. 1

It follows that

> from this perspective, then, we can understand
> man's terrifying violence as deriving from the
> behavior of the predatory animal, whose
> characteristic he came to acquire in the course
> of becoming man.

Man, then, is a killer who must kill in order to live. It is at once the most ancient and most fundamental part of his nature.

Ethologists have noted the prevalence of aggression among peoples regardless of their stage of cultural advancement of retardation.

> There are certainly cultural differences in
> human aggression. But convincing proof that
> any group is wholly lacking in aggressive
> behavior has not yet been produced.....Nor do
> primitive and culturally advanced peoples seem
> to differ fundamentally in their aggressive
> disposition. 2

If there were any peoples who did not share this aggression, they must have soon disappeared, for the necessity of finding food would have eliminated them.[3] Man is 40,000 years old. For the first 30,000 years he was a hunter-gatherer. Even gatherers who survived chiefly on roots and berries have been known to kill small animals. A few hunter-gatherers survived into the modern world, notably the pygmies, the Eskimo, the bushmen and the Australian aborigines. Killing animals for food laid down a tendency and accumulated a left-over drive, which became habitual.

Hunting as a practice has been studied by Ortega y Gasset, the Spanish philosopher. In his view it has a very special meaning, for it asserts that the food chain is an hierarchy; that is the essence of his message.

> Hunting is what an animal does to take
> possession, dead or alive, of some other
> being that belongs to a species basically
> inferior to its own. 4

There is no democracy in nature alive, but there is a balance.

Hunting as a way of life has its effects on the hunter. It serves to keep him primitive, to insure that his basic nature will not stray too far from the life-death cycle. For man took an unpredictable turn when he stumbled (as he must have) on the device of artifacts. The use of tools and signs raised his position considerably and suddenly over other and often much larger and stronger animals.

In the words of Dr. Allen B. Rothballer, "Man appears to have evolved as a predator, and now belongs among the more aggressive species. With improvements in technology and energy sources, he has become increasingly more dangerous, yet his aggressive-controlling mechanisms appear never to have been particularly well developed".[5]

Thomas Carlyle once observed that "Man is a tool-using animal. Without tools he is nothing". As his brain developed in size and complexity, so did his tools. Early man probably used wood tools as the higher apes do. Then he graduated to stone. Stone survived better, hence our conception of the Early Stone Age. When he discovered animal husbandry, he passed

> from being essentially a hunter to being
> essentially a shepherd -- that is to say, to
> a semistationary way of life. Very soon he
> turned from shepherd to farmer, and became
> completely stationary. The use of his legs,
> his lungs, his senses of smell, of orientation,
> of the winds, of the trails, all diminish....As
> he perfected his weapons he ceased to be wild....
> Today's best-trained hunter cannot begin to
> compare his form with that of the sylvan actions
> of his remote counterpart, Palaeolithic man.
> Progress in weaponry is somewhat compensated by
> regress in the form of the hunter. 6

But remember, the instinct of the hunter remained. He found himself essentially in his present predicament: leading a sedentary life while possessed of all the violent instincts of the hunter, which were sure to find another outlet.

"The human body is about 40% muscle".[7] Man was not born to a sedentary existence, and he does not take well to it. It is necessary therefore "to make the concept of activity the central point of any system of ideas about life". As any neurophysiologist will tell you, the involvement of the cortex in the motor area is extensive. The frustration of the use of the musculature to its fullest extent must therefore have important consequences to the whole animal.[8]

No wonder, then, that killing comes naturally to man. It was his oldest daily practice, and was probably in this way built into the genes He could not give it up without a price, for his muscles had become accoustomed to violent action, to extreme effort, and must suffer when frustrated or inhibited.

I am not of course suggesting any such thing as an inherited memory, but if the brain does not retain any evidence of the prevalence of the practice of killing, the muscles do. In the process of evolution, those with the strongest muscles and the largest frames to support them would have survived, the other would have perished. Thus there evolved the professional killer whose skills were needed by all.

Unlike most other animals, man eats nearly everything, for he is an herbivore as well as a carnivore. When the ice ages, which are known to have lasted for some time, prevailed, men ate the other animals, for there could not have been much edible vegetation. Is this why the largest animals perished and why man survived? Ice in the northern countries is still known to account for frozen ground to a depth of 1000 feet. There is nothing to eat above the perma-frost for nothing grows. Eskimos survive by fishing, which of course is a form of hunting and is the one still prevalent with us, because of the refuge the sea provides for the fish, small as well as large.

The killing of animals served more than one purpose. The recurrent ice ages and the existence of man in northern climates meant that he also needed clothing to survive, and must have dressed in the skins of the animals he killed. Both the need for warmth and the need for food thus encouraged the practice of killing. No other activity could have competed with this one; it called on all his energies, for the small animals were swifter than he was and the large ones were stronger. Thus his ingenuity as well as his strength must have been cultivated by hunting.

A simple comparison between man and the other animals with respect to the organic drives will be very revealing. In them when a need has been satisfied, the drive subsides. A lion which has just killed and eaten a deer lies down in the midst of the herd without disturbing it. In man, however, the drive does not stop when a need is reduced, for he antici- pates that it will recur. Though he has just killed a cow and eaten some of the soft parts, he knows that his hunger will return, and so he breeds cattle and builds ranches and butcher shops against his future needs.

Every hunter who ever went after big game, such as lions and tigers, knows that the hunter is also the hunted. In hunting such as this there is always the risk of being killed and eaten. It was a mutual arrange- ment, when the advantage was shifted suddenly to the hunters because of their new and more powerful weapons.

The difference between man and the other animals is crucial. For the pattern of difference is repeated for each of the needs. When an animal is thirsty, it looks for water, but once having drunk, that is the end of it until later on when thirst manifests itself again. Man, on the other hand, learned to anticipate his needs and so took measures to provide for them in the future.

This gave him one enormous advantage. He arranged for the inheritance of artifacts, those material objects altered through human agency for human uses. The other animals make artifacts, too, for instance birds build nests, beavers construct dams, but they never pass them on to the young, who must when the time comes build their own.

The life of man as a hunter came to an end when he invented artifacts, which enabled him to solve the hunger problem without resorting to the chase. History in fact begins with artifacts; before that there was only the routine of hunting as a matter of daily survival. Artifacts changed the picture because they enabled him to surmount the problem of arranging for future need-reductions. Knowing that thirst is sure to return, man builds reservoirs, conduits and purification plants. In order to meet the demands of hunger, he learned how to erect fences and plant crops, and with these he positioned himself permanently. No longer a nomad compelled to follow the seasonal migration of the herds, he constructed houses near his farms and made roads between them.

When at the end of the last Ice Age, the receding ice-cap left the world for man to inhabit, the result was the transition from hunter to agriculturalist, from migratory nomad to city-dweller, the most decisive change in all of human history. It occurred only a few millennia ago, and it resulted in a population growth which multiplied some sixteen times between 8000 and 4000 BC.

Being human is a condition which provides a high contrast but exacts some heavy penalties. Let us look at two of the consequences.

The first is that the various structures erected to satisfy one need or another have together led to a new and almost wholly artificial environment. Man has become a builder, and the result is that with the cities he inhabits all over the world he has made for himself a built environment. Since man is a product of the genotype interacting with the environment, it is too early to say what kind of human being will result when generations or city-dwellers have occurred. In transforming his immediate environment he may have transformed himself. Civilization, which is nothing more nor less than the standing arrangements of arti-facts intended to reduce future organic needs, has resulted from generations of the efforts of homo faber, a comparatively recent development.

The second consequence following man's anticipation of his recurring needs may be called the problem of the left-over drives. Killing for food was part of the routine life of primitive man, a daily affair of violence in his world; he knew no other. It is no longer a necessity for most individuals, since it has been institutionalized and so provided for. But the drive is still there: the killing that has been a habit for many millions of years will not subside so easily. Indeed the evidence is that it has not lessened at all. Man the killer remains a killer still. Violence is excluded from the sedentary life but returns to claim its own.

The result is that man seeks other channels to reduce his need for violent action, and finds it in war. The killing of men by other men is nothing new.

As Burkert observes,

> it is as easy, or even easier, to kill a man
> as it is to kill a fleeing beast, so that from
> earliest times men slipped repeatedly into
> cannibalism. Thus from the very start, self-
> destruction was a threat to the human race. 9

Man the predator is with us still. The killing and eating of animals was not one of the ways primitive man kept himself alive, it was the only way. Killing was an essential part of his ordinary life, just as it is today, only now it is assigned to surrogates, leaving the majority with the mistaken impression that they have no association with killers.

No doubt the orderly and institutionally established social provisions of killing animals for food leaves most individuals with an anciently inherited but now largely unused habit of killing. For most peaceful and law-abiding citizens, this habit is frustrated routinely

until it is almost forgotten; but in a few it continues on and has its
effects. These few are the so-called criminal types, those who commit
murders for one reason or another, and so constitute what has been called
"the subculture of violence".[10]

Those like Freud who would suppose a "death instinct" as opposed to a
"life instinct", or like Konrad Lorenz who thinks that aggression is always
the result of a particular frustration, are ignoring the positive basis of
the drive in an organic need. People do not simply 'behave', they always
behave about something, and in this case that something is food. That is
not the only organic need resulting in violence: competition for females
will do just as well, or for an economic or political advantage. But
probably the life of the hunter, which was the life of early man for many
thousands of years, provides all of the motive we will need to account for
violence.

When cities emerged there arose in human life in a quite natural way
an ambivalent motivation: building cities to provide for all future needs,
and tearing them down in wars. Obviously these two drives cannot be
satisfied at one and the same time, so there has developed a sort of
rhythm of building and destroying, periods of peace when civilizations
advance, streets are paved and houses filled with artifacts of art and
technology; then periods of war when cities are burned and bombed, people
are killed, and much of what they have made is destroyed. We have not
changed the essential picture, only increased the volume, due to an
enormous escalation in population.

The examination of primitive societies in an effort to understand
human aggression has its limits and I can see no easy answer. There is
a qualitative as well as a quantitative difference between such societies

and the societies of advanced cultures and civilizations. The hunter-
gatherers did little to disturb the environment in five million years. In
the 10,000 years of civilization, however, the situation was changed
radically by the introduction and profusion of artifacts, which are so
varied, so large and complex, that together they provided a new environment.

What has become of aggression under these new circumstances? Has it
been suppressed or increased? That is the important question.

Unfortunately, the basic drives have not changed with the changing of
human circumstances. The food chain is not to be gain-said, and it is
responsible for the killing instinct, which will be there as long as hunger
exists. Man is no longer alone in the forest with the wild animals he can
kill and eat, he is now a citizen in a large metropolis, with some people
specialized to do his killing for food for him. Yet he has retained the
ingrained tendencies of the hunters his ancestors were, only with no
outlet.

The natural man is a hunting man and the Palaeolithic in man is still
with us. For in periods of peace (as though war was not enough) man takes
a "vacation from the human condition" by "escaping from the present to
that pristine form of being a man".[11] And of what precisely does that
consist? Why, in hunting and fishing, both techniques of killing. In the
case of the larger animals food even is no longer a valid excuse; it is
the killing pure and simple which occupies him, for on one eats eagle or
lion. Every year still in the 1980s from June until October tarpon rodeos
are held in the Gulf of Mexico despite the fact that the fish is inedible.
It comes down to this, that the desire to get rid of wars is not as
strong as the desire to fight them. The killing instinct is too deep in

people to allow peace to be an easy solution. Wars do fill a human need.

Thus we have a standoff and one suddenly rendered impossible by a rise in the efficiency of weapons. It has become a game which in the ordinary course of things we can no longer play. Nuclear war is a terminal prospect in which there are no winners, only losers.

What then can we do when we find that the problem is ourselves? The need to kill, inherited from ancient hunting cultures, is deep in every one. It can no longer be tolerated, and so we are backed up to the problem of how to change our own human nature, something we are not disposed to undertake. 'Physician heal thyself' is advice no doctor takes seriously.

I once saw a school bus on its way home in the late afternoon. Most of the children in it had been delivered safely, all, that is, except two little boys; and in that large and empty vehicle they were alone, and fighting!

The progress of civilization is marked only by an increase in intensification. We do what we have always done: help and hurt our fellow man, an ambivalent motivation which because it is contradictory is in the end self-defeating. There has been no progress in motivation.

Perhaps we will not be able to understand war until we learn to accept the meaning of peace. Life itself is involved with death in a terrible struggle, for we are still moved by the needs of prehistoric man. A long quiet period in any society only serves to bring on its opposite, which in any case was inevitable.

Meanwhile the killing goes on. In this sense history is a record of human failure. The killer is today in our huge populations something of a specialist. There is the individual killer and there is the social killer. The former is typically a psychopath, the latter a patriot.

The essence of the problem is easy to restate: killing is a left-over drive, one presenting a formidable obstacle to the peaceful aims of man the builder. When we say that homo faber is opposed by homo necans, we are taking about the same man.

Notes

1 Walter Burkert, Homo Necans, Peter Bing trans. (Berkeley, CA 1983, University of California Press), p. 17.

2 Irenäus Eibl-Eibesfeldt, Love and Hate, G. Strachan trans. (London 1971, Methuen), p. 71. The author's view that the aggressive drive is balanced by his tendency to altruistic behavior except in a single instance has no support from the facts.

3 J. K. Anderson, Hunting In The Ancient World (London 1985, University of California Press).

4 Jose Ortega y Gasset, Meditations of Hunting, H. B. Wescott, trans. (New York 1972, Charles Scribner's Sons), p. 57. Much of this treatise seems to be an anachronism, for it celebrates in hunting the joy of once again experiencing what it must have been like many thousands of years ago to be a primitive.

5 "Aggression, Defense and Neurohumors" in C. B. Clamente and D. B. Lindsley (eds.), Aggression and Defense (Berkeley 1967, University of California Press), p. 148.

6 Ibid., p. 121.

7 J. Z. Young, An Introduction to The Study of Man (Oxford 1971, The Clarendon Press), p. 87

8 C. Eyzaguirrie and S. J. Fidone, Physiology of The Nervous System (Chicago 1975, Year Book Medical Publishers).

9 Op. cit., p. 18.

10 Marvin E. Wolfgang and Franco Ferracuti, The Subculture of Violence (London 1967, Tavistock Publications).

11 Ortega y Gasset, Ibid., p. 134.

Chapter 3

THE CANNIBALS

Cannibalism, the eating of human flesh, is a new name for a very old practice. The name is derived from a corruption of 'Carib', and the Caribs, who were man-eaters, were discovered in the West Indies no more than a century ago.[1]

Cannibalism has had a long history.[2] Sir Charles Fliot has recorded that certain sects in India, which were quite old, the Kapalikas or Kalamukhas, "carried skulls and ate the flesh of corpses".[3]

The practice of cannibalism was not unknown to Aristotle. In the Nicomachean Ethics he reported that "some of the tribes about the Black Sea that have gone savage are said to delight —— in raw meat or in human flesh, or in lending their children to one another to feast upon".[4]

It was not unknown, either, to Chrysippus in the third century BC who wrote that it was permitted to eat the corpses of the dead.[5]

Perhaps the best and most comprehensive account of cannibalism is Garry Hogg's Cannibalism and Human Sacrifice.[6] He is concerned chiefly with recouting the cannibalism practiced by many tribes still today or until comparatively recent times, such as the Fiji Islanders, the Kwakiutl Indians, the tribes in the Amazon Basin, Nigeria, Sierra Leone, the Congo Basin, Indonesia, New Guinea, Melanesia, Polynesia, the Australian aborignes and the Maori of New Zealand.

It must be for the victims a severely painful way to die; but at the same time the pain is incidental: the killing is done for quite another reason. Various methods have been employed to prepare the victims; usually a knife is the weapon, but many have been boiled alive. Once the victim dies there is no more interest; but in torture, by comparison, the pain inflicted is the central aim.

Cannibalism still exists in odd corners, though without the approval of any large and established society; yet it must be as old as the human species itself. That is why it deserves consideration in a book devoted to the underside of human nature.

The four most enduring practices are cannibalism, astrology, slavery and prostitution...I shall deal in this chapter only with cannibalism, reserving the discussion of slavery for chapter 7. I might mention here, however, that astrology and prostitution still flourish. Astrology is practiced among us despite the falsity of its claims.[7] As for prostitution, it is legal in the state of Nevada but endemic almost everywhere.

I hope to show here that cannibalism while universally banned and classified as a crime, remains close beneath the daily affairs of human life, always ready to surface at the behest of hunger in any extreme form.

There is a tendency to learn only from those who see mankind in the most favorable light. All references to cannibalism, except as an abhorrent custom practiced by those who are not yet civilized, are put aside as not relevant to the human situation except as an historical aberration. For those who are willing to confront the truth without flinching, the facts argue otherwise.

All organisms, except the lowest, exist by killing and consuming other organisms below them in the food chain. Man at the top of the hierarchy is poised above it, and therefore the natural predator of all organic species, including the animals. What activity has occupied him longer on a daily

basis than killing for food? It is unnatural to expect him to do otherwise. Cannibalism is merely the recognition that his fellow men are also
animals and therefore potentially sources of the satisfaction of hunger.
Any rejection of this source must be on other grounds, humanitarian and
altruistic, for instance. But what need, when push comes to shove, can
compete with hunger? That all we do is to keep cannibalism in check is
shown by the fact that in unusual situations when other food is unobtain-
able, as in a shipwreck or an airplane crash, it bursts out once more.

All three activities: astrology and prostitution as well as
cannibalism, still exist today despite the enlightenment provided by the
humanities; and although few persons approve, many still have recourse to
them; which only goes to show that the great age and long following of an
institution is no endorsement of it. Cannibalism in fact seems abhorrent
to most people who do not understand that under different circumstances,
while they might continue to be opposed, they might also be compelled to
participate. Judged by such evidence as we can accumulate from the
accidental isolation of groups, cannibalism is for everyone only some ten
days away. There are, as we shall see, those who might be called
'cannibals by force of circumstances', and that could well include any of
us.

Cannibalism is no stranger to the natural world. It is to be found in
many other species, many of which are much older than man. That in fact
cannibalism in the lower species is quite common has been noted.[8] In no
less than some 1,300 species it is often the cause of the morality of the
species. The same authority also notes that cannibalism has been
recorded in some 60 human societies, where it was "often the second most
important item of dietary protein".

In discussing "the rooted bellicosity of human nature, William James described man as "biologically considered...the most formidable of all the beasts of prey, and indeed, the only one that preys systematically on its own species".[9] He has pointed out that cannibalism is what distinguishes man from the other primates.

As early finds increase together with the technological means of examining them, the evidence grows that earliest man was a cannibal. "Many of the long bones found in the [Choukoutien caves near Peking] have been split open. Since only man can split bones open, — to get at the marrow other animals chew the bones — we are forced to conclude that the Old Stone Age men of the Peking caves were addicted to cannibalism".[10] A. C. Blanc has shown that in a range of fossil skills from the mid-Pleistocene onwards "a careful and symmetric incising of the periphery of the foramen magnum to produce an opening which, on comparative evidence was made for the practice of extracting the brain for eating".[11]

Early man had to pursue and kill animals in order to eat and so survive. But his efforts were not confined to other animals.

> Skulls of Australopithicines have been found
> showing a form of fracture consisting of two
> depressions close together. The humerus bone
> of antelopes have been discovered nearby. The
> end of such a bone fits well into the skull
> depressions. In other words, a million years
> ago people were already hit on the head by
> other people. 12

Professor Blanc noted that ritual theophagy must have had its origins in a former ritual cannibalism, perpetuated, symbolically at least, in the Roman Catholic rite of the Eucharist.

According to Grahame Clark, the Lower and Middle Paleolithic hunters were cannibals, human "long bones were normally split exactly as were those of wild animals to facilitate the extraction of marrow, and the

aperture at the base of the skull had habitually been enlarged in just the
same way as among the Melanesians of recent times who favored human brain
as a delicacy".[13] Moreover, "certain discoveries from the closing phase of
the last Interglacial seem indeed to indicate the continuance of
cannibalism, notably the Neaderthal skull from Monte Circea, Italy...and
the mass find at Krapina in Yugoslavis".[14]

Gernet reports that in the Sung capital at Hangchow there was a
restaurant specializing in dishes cooked from human flesh.[15]

Sir Richard Burton, the English explorer, traveling in central Africa
in 1858, found two tribes of man-eaters. It was not an unusual experience
even in those late days.[16] There are many accounts of shipwrecked sailors
eating their weakest companions or those who died. A well documented case
is that of four sailors who killed and ate one who became ill.[17]

Cannibalism in the Marquesa Islands northeast of Tahiti was a well
known practice and survived into modern times. Thor Heyerdahl and his
bride found ample evidence when they visited Fatu-Hiva in 1973, as they
have recorded in their book of discovery,[18] and may have known personally
the last of those natives who dined on human flesh. It may have been out
of necessity, as the only available source of protein.

In every war there are acocunts of isolated men who without food felt
obliged by the severe pangs of hunger to eat the bodies of the dead. But
it could happen in peace time, too. Perhaps the best known and most ably
recorded of examples of cannibalism in modern times is the account of the
Uruguayan rugby team from Montevideo whose airplane crashed in the high
Andes while on a charter flight to Chile.[19] The account is very detailed;
the qualms and revulsions natural to civilized people occupied them at
first; but hunger is stronger than any belief however fundamental, or

any other impulse including the most basic repugnance; and so the
survivors cut off slices of the dead companions who lay around them and ate
them raw.

A hunger that triumphed after ten days of starvation, that is the
essence of the story. There were many precedents. On January 5, 1807, a
gale-driven sloop, the Nautilus, hit an uncharted reef in the Aegean.
Most of the crew scrambled onto a low rock. On the evening of the fourth
day the survivors cut up a corpse and ate it. Such situations were not
rare in accounts of shipwreck. In 1184 four shipwrecked English sailors
lived without food in a lifeboat for 24 days. When one became ill, the
captain killed him and the survivors drank his blood, butchered his body
and ate it.[20] In the mid-nineteenth century the Donner party migrating
West in covered wagons got stranded by blizzards in the snows of the
Sierra Nevada mountains and were reduced to eating those who died.[21]

Cannibalism is a topic difficult for most to accept, but there are
exceptions. When a young Brazilian journalist visited Jan Sibelius, the
composer, in Finland and told him there were still cannibals in the
interior who ate missionaries, he is reported to have been delighted.
"How splendid that there are still cannibals", he said.[22]

In the islands to the west of New Guinea and Australia, for instance
the Solomon Islands and Fiji Islands, cannibalism was an established
practice. It has evidently also always existed in parts of Africa.[23]

The random accounts of travelers for centuries attests to the
persistent custom of eating people. The ancient Aztecs certainly were
ritual cannibals.[24] The seventeenth century descriptions of the coast of
Brazil report cannibalism among the Tupinambas.[25] The practice at the
time was certainly not confined to them.[26]

There have always been many travellers accounts of cannibalism among primitive people and the practice still exists today in the more inaccessible regions. For example in a sequestered gorge of the Murray River in the Blucher range the natives made it a practice to cook and eat the bodies of slain enemies.[27] Cannibalism was not unknown to other parts of New Guinea, either.[28]

Cannibalism survives in isolated tribes and remote regions far from most contemporary influences, chiefly in Asia and Africa. It is probably disappearing as a conventional practice.[29]

It has not been a favorite topic with anthropologists or social investigators generally, probably because of the revulsion most civilized people feel about it. Still, it persists in various isolated pockets of primitive tribes. Idi Amin of Uganda is said to have practiced ritual cannibalism.[30] Indeed it can occur still whenever and wherever people, whatever their beliefs, find themselves alive but without sufficient food. "Evidence before the courts showed that Japanese medical officers removed hearts and livers from healthy prisoners while they were still alive. The cannibalism of Allied prisoners was authorized when other food was not available".[31]

In a word, all of us are capable of practicing cannibalism should the extreme conditions which bring it about arise. This is something we ought to know concerning ourselves when we come to an impartial examination of human nature.

Notes

1 Science, 144, 502 (1964).
2 Perhaps the oldest reference to cannibalism is in Aristotle's Nichomachean Ethics, 1148b20-25. Cf. also Garry Hogg, Cannibalism and Human Sacrifice (London 1958, Robert Haley); also George Fitzhugh, Cannibals All (Cambridge, Mass., 1960, Belknap Press).
3 Hinduism and Buddhism (London 1921, Routledge & Kegan Paul), 3 vols., vol. 2, p. 203.

4 1148b20-24.

5 Diogenes Laertius, Lives of Eminent Philosophers, R. D. Hicks trans. (London 1925, William Heinemann), 2 vols., vol. 2, p. 297.

6 (London 1958, Robert Hale Ltd.).

7 See e. g. Shawn Carlson, "A Double-blind Test of Astrology" in Nature, 318, 419-425, especially the conclusion of p. 425.

8 J. S. Jones, in Nature, 299, 202 (1982).

9 Memories and Studies (London 1911, Longmans Green & Co.), p. 301.

10 A. C. Blanc, "Some Evidence for the Ideologies of Early Man" in Social Life of Early Man edited by S. L. Washburn (Chicago 1961, Viking Fund Publications in Anthropology, No. 31.

11 World Prehistory (Cambridge 1969, University Press), p. 39.

12 Richard Fiennes, Bones, Bodies and Disease

13 World Prehistory (Cambridge 1969, University Press), p. 39.

14 Op. cit., p. 45

15 K. C. Chang (ed.) Food in Chinese Culture (New Haven 1977, Yale University Press).

16 The Lake Regions of Central Africa (New York 1961, Horizon Press), 2 vols., vol. 1, pp. 114, 123.

17 A. W. Brian Simpson, Cannibalism and The Common Law (Chicago 1985, Chicago University Press).

18 Fatu-Hiva (New York 1976, New American Library), pp. 117-18, 183, 121, 217018.

19 Piers Paul Read, Alive: The Story of the Andes Survivors (London 1974, Secker & Warburg).

20 A. W. Brian Simpson, Cannibalism and The Common Law (Chicago 1985, University Press). The title stems from a famous trial which followed and hung on the issue of whether cannibalistic homocide constituted murder.

21 Clay Blair Jr., Survive! (London 1974, Mayflower).

22 Santeri Levas, Sibelius (London 1972, J. M. Dent), p. 35.

23 John Lord, Honor, Duty and Empire: The Life of Colonel Minertzhagen

24 Bernal Diaz del Castillo, Conquest of New Spain, chapter 3.

25 Handbook of South American Indians

26 Louis Ange Pitou, Voyage a Cayenne dans les deux Ameriques et chez les Anthropophages (Paris 1807).

27 Malcolm S. Kirk, New York Times, January 1, 1973.

28 "The Asmat of New Guinea: Head-Hunters in Today's World", the National Geographic, 141, 376-409 (1972).

29 Cf. e. g. J. A. Hunter, Hunter (New York 1952, Harper & Row) pp. 151-2; Jean-Pierre Hallet, Congo Kitabu (New York 1966, Random House), chapter 4; George Fithugh, Cannibals All (Cambridge, Mass., 1960, Belknap Press of Harvard University Press).

30 Cf. George Ivan Smith, Ghosts of Kampala (London 1980, pp. 111-12.

31 Philip R. Piccigallo, The Japanese on Trial: Allied War Crimes Operations in the East 1945-1951 (Austin 1979, p. 27, quoted in Paul Johnson, op. cit., p. 428.

Chapter 4

THE WARRIORS 1

War may be defined as the planned killing of the members of one society
by those of another, the extension of conflict into extreme violence between
peoples organized in political units. War, understood as collective
aggression, has been around a long time, so long that It has become familiar.
Despite this fact, it is treated by most men of good will as though it were
an intruder and usurper. It involves the utmost use by the state of all the
powers of forceful action which were turned over to it initially by
individuals; it is not the only kind of conflict, as anyone who has engaged
in economic competition knows, but it is the most destructive; and it is one
of the most promient products of civilization.

Much has happened in the world to change cultural conditions since
Quincy Wright published his masterly work A Study of War.[1] Thanks to many
developments, from new doctrine to new technologies, there are now new
problems. Transportation and communication have advanced so quickly that
the whole world has become a very small place, and what happens anywhere
may affect what happens anywhere else. There are no longer any isolated
communities except at ground level. The air carries not only airplanes but
also missles, and not only these but electronic messages and observations
from satellites and the space shuttle capable of revealing from miles up
conditions on the surface of the globe and even below it.

In a word, it really is 'one world' with interconnections of all sorts both actual and potential between any one place and any other. That makes an armed struggle however local in character everybody's business because it may have reverberations world-wide. That we all live in the same world subject to the same events is easy to say but more difficult to conceive. The old parochial viewpoint is with us still despite the considerable knowledge that it no longer represents the facts. Our experience goes back a few generations, while the future carries the possibilities of events that wIll not fit with it. We are in a sense, then, helpless when confronting not only the future but the present.

Under these conditions, what happens to war? We have to face the fact first of all that the ordinary understanding is misleading. It assures us that wars are uncommon events nobody wants and that they are usually provoked by outsiders. That is what many always believe, though there is little truth to it.

The truth is that wars are quite ordinary occurences. There are few periods in history when there were no wars. Peter Sorokin has examined the history of eleven European countries for some eight hundred years and found them to have been engaged in military action 47% of the time.[2] In our own time the situation has greatly worsened. Wars currently are being fought on every continent, and the greatest war of all is threatened. War must be the most familiar kind of enterprise because one or more is always in progress.

Wars are in fact so common that even in this day of high publicity, universal reporting and mass media, some go almost unnoticed. How many citizens of the United States knew at the time about the persistent conflict between the royalists and Egyptians in the Yemen? How many were aware of the civil war in progress between Nigeria and the secessionist province of Biafra?

No one seems much inclined to believe that war is a familiar affair and natural to the human species. It is usually treated as a variety of aberrant behavior, an extreme form of aggression; but in fact it occurs everywhere and among all sorts of cultures in various stages of social and material development.

Considering how much travel and exploration had taken place by Europeans on a global dimension from the Renaissance on: vast continents explored, and even empires carved out, ending with the British Empire and the Pax Britannica, it is somewhat amazing how very provincial the European thinkers remained. When examining issues of war and peace, of conflicts between peoples and the hopes for their resolution, they wrote as though Europe was the only consideration. Kant seems for example to have had in mind behind his dreams of improvement only the Europeans.

War is organized usually by governments though not always or necessarily, it can also be a spontaneous effort by citizens, as happened in the American Revolution of 1776. Hobbes alone with his bellum omnium contra omnes assumed that war is the usual condition, whether being waged or not, with peace only an interruption. But as Wright correctly pointed out, war and peace are extreme conditions which allow for many intermediate states of agreement or hostility. The current relations between the United States and the Soviet Union, which have been characterized as those of a "cold war", furnish an apt example.

The now classic treatise by Karl von Clausewitz On War, with its famous statement that "war is nothing but the continuity of state policy by other means", assumed that the practice of war is an established institution, one that has always existed and is here to stay. That is a devastating assumption to all those who had thought otherwise. It certainly must have reinforced the views of Marx and Lenin and of Mao Zedong. The acceptance of war as a fact of life means that all those who practice it recognize its necessity. They must be responding to something deep in human nature, as indeed they are; something as deep perhaps as the desire for peace.

War is after all also the recognition between two peoples (two nations, two tribes) that they have some common ground. They meet and do battle for something they hold in common, and because they are at the same cultural level, they represent a common concern. The larger wars, those between groups of nations, for example the two 'world wars', is evidence that something larger exists which they have in common. Star wars, a misnomer, by the way, for global missile defense, is clear evidence that large wars between groups of nations have no well-defined boundaries and perhaps no boundaries at all. Wars represent common interests even though diminishing them.

War is the great leveler; it reduces all human relations to a common denominator: the appeal to physical force as the criterion of all decision-making. War, Wright says, is only the name for "a very large-scale resort to violence".[3] That is the all-out conception, though many intermediate forms of conflict also exist. The battle of ideals has to be counted also, with the outcome dependent on which ideals prevail by being put into practice; a justification, so to speak, judged by success. In many previous wars the loser of a battle ceded a province, but that does not explain why the Goths sacked Rome in 499 BC or how the Christians finally overcame the Romans in the third and fourth centuries AD. Human beings interact at many levels, from the ground level of brute force to the top level of consciously-held abstract ideas, and only the former can legitimately use the term, war, though the effects in the end may be the same whatever the weapons.

Who is to say by what a war is provoked? Wars are fought by people, not without them. What is taken as a cause depends upon when you choose to date the events. Reading cause-and-effect backward from the present, it is always possible to make an arbitrary stop. Besides, it all depends upon the assumptions as to what constituted a provocation.

A list of the reasons why wars have been fought include most of the motives that activate people generally. There are wars to gain territory, to eliminate a threat to national borders, to further the cause of this or that religion, to gain power, "to make the world safe for democracy", to bring about the socialist ideal of the Marxists, to gain an economic advantage, to "civilize" natives, to avoid becoming the slavery victims of a conquest, as an alternative to the monotony of peace, and many more.

It is interesting and perhaps revealing that in Quincy Wright's Study of War a different list is offered. "Wars usually result", we are told,

> because of the need of political power confronted
> by rivals continually to increase itself in order
> to survive, because of the tendency of a system of
> law to assume that the state is completely sovereign,
> because of the utility of external war as a means of
> integrating societies in times of emergency, and
> because persons cannot satisfy the human disposition
> to dominate except through identification with a
> sovereign group. 4

No doubt these are true accounts; and I would point out that the two lists hardly overlap. We must probe more deeply if we wish to understand the fundamental nature of the human animal, and so I have saved some of the most telling causes for the last.

Economic competition is one of the most familiar. "The struggle for wealth, power and prestige is a constant feature". Again, "the feeling of belonging to a group ... requires some measure of antagonism to other groups".[5]

One of the more common causes is in the pretension to the possession of the absolute truth. If a state thinks it has that, there is no choice left but to seek to impose it on others —— always, of course, for their own good! Given two or more such states, war is inevitable; even with one, there could be organized military resistance. For the absolute truth may be one of political economy —— as with the Soviet Union or of religion —— as with Islam —— but it does not matter since the result will be the same. According to Muslim law, for example, the world is divided into a domain of Islam and a domain of war. Had the entire world embraced Islam, we are told, this second domain would not have been necessary, but under the circumstances of resistance to conversion, it is. Any war conducted in the interest of an absolute truth is regarded by those waging it as a just war.

Too many different reasons have been given traditionally for us to see any cause for war they could have in common. War is certainly a familiar kind of human behavior, a traditional phenomenon of the species. We are not in possession of a sufficient amount of information to know whether war is a form of human self-destruction, like that of the lemmings in Norway, or whether it is a natural process for keeping the population down to a subsistence level. No countries which engage in periodic wars are in danger of out-breeding their food supply. This has been true for so long that even now, when we can provide for any given population by means of industrial agriculture, the practice of war is preserved.

It is fashionable both to condemn war as inhuman and to wage it in the national interest. For there exists not only actual wars but also what

Hobbes called a disposition to war which prevails in time of peace,
occasioned by disvalues: by fraud, falsehood, and fear, fed by competition,
diffidence and the hope of glory. I want to add to the disposition the
incentives of force illegally used, lies deliberately perpetrated, and fear
purposely inculcated.

People often do the same things though they profess to do them for
different reasons. Evidently, there is always a moral justification for
war. The base for it exists in the deep-rooted belief in an inherent
superiority. Every people, every nation, seeks to impose its morality
upon others, on the well-intentioned ground that its morality is the
universal morality. In this way it seeks to justify its acquisitive
aggression.

The moral justification is usually contained in the assumption of the
conquerors that conquest will be good for all of the conquered or for some
chosen sector. The Romans took it for granted that any country which came
under the domination of the Empire would be better off because of the
stable government from which it would benefit and the properity which
would ensue. It was the firm belief of the leaders of the Ottoman Empire
that to compel a defeated people to accept Islam or the sword was to do
what was best for them. And today the Russian communists really believe
that they are liberating an oppressed proletariat, and this remains their
faith even when that proletariat enjoys a standard of living greater than
that which prevails in the Soviet Union.

It is difficult to take seriously the reasons which are given for wars
when we see how readily the sides can be changed. In 1512, Henry VIII
allied England with the Hapsburgs against France. Three years later he
rallied England with France against the Hapsburgs. Seven years after that

he allied England with the Hapsburgs against France again. Yet no one seemed to think his behavior in this respect extraordinary. In point of fact it was not.

More recent examples are not hard to come by. In 1914 Italy and Japan joined with France and Great Britain against Germany. In 1939 Italy and Japan joined with Germany against France and Great Britain. Shifts in foreign policy, including such complete reversals, are not necessarily the result of whim or perfidy. There are more variables in social affairs than anyone has yet understood, and the man of action is obliged by his ignorance to make continual reassessments of the forces involved and to feel his way, and this uncertain process requires him in all honesty sometimes to reverse himself or his country's historic commitments.

All those who seek the causes of war usually think that for any war there must always have been a single cause. This assumption overlooks two facts: that there is a distinction between effect and cause, and that for any one conflict there may have been multiple causes.

Occasions are usually surface events which precipitate conflicts, such as the murder of the archduke at Sarajevo or Hitler's invasion of Poland; whereas causes lie deeper. In the former case, it was national rivalries, and in the latter, one step in the Nazi plan to conquer Europe. Probably deeper than these events still lay personal rivalries, racial differences, and many more catalogued and uncatalogued.

Social events, such as wars, are complex affairs, as complex as human life itself, and so multiple causation is not the exception but the rule. As Shakespeare pointed out in Hamlet, men will go to war for an eggshell when honor's at the stake. It is entirely misleading that at the present time thanks to the advanced development of biology and the slower

development of sociology, the individual seems much more complex than
society. This is only because we know more about him than we do about
society. Societies must be more complex than their parts, which are human
individuals.

We know little or nothing as yet about the complex composition of
societies when we consider that the artifacts which connect individuals and
different social groups have never been included. Moreover, organizations
of individuals acting in concert almost never behave like those same
individuals when acting separately. These relations have never been
explained though there is nothing secret about them; all is conducted in
the full daylight of exposure to reason and the disclosure of fact. That
is the deep problem of those who would outlaw war and who have failed to
do so time and again. Human behavior cannot be properly regulated until it
is well understood; that this is true even for peaceful pursuits has not
been recognized.

Settled civilizations having an abundance of goods are less inclined to
wage wars than their more deprived neighbors who see a possible advantage
in conquests. This is obviously not the whole story, not so long as an
economic advantage can be clothed in crusading religious zeal. The wars of
religion in the 16th and 17th centuries gave way to wars of nationalism in
the 19th and 20th centuries, and now seem to be giving way to wars of
secular politics (the struggle between liberal democracy and Marxist
totalitarianism).

Although not generally acknowledged by men of good will, it is none
the less true that to many (though certainly not to all) the thrill of
combat is greater than any other. Living is never so wonderful as when
one is facing death. As an American veteran of world war 2, a gentle

mathematician whose life had been spent in the classroom, said after due
reflection, "There is no ecstasy like battle". "More ecstatic than sex with
a woman you love and who loves you?" "Yes, even more than that", he
insisted, "a deep satisfaction worth all the risk of being maimed or killed".

Have there been any justifiable wars, any wars which have resulted in
lasting good effects? This question, often asked, is a difficult one to
answer because we are never in possession of all the facts and so not able to
make a final assessment. The Peloponnesian Wars which Sparta won destroyed
the best of Greek culture and almost marked the end of its achievement. On
the other hand, the Asian conquests of Alexander the Great probably were
responsible for the fact that any of Greek culture survived into modern world
by making a Roman inheritance possible.

Wars at the time always seem to bring out the worst in everyone. Would
it be possible to argue that wars are won more by those who are willing and
even eager to practice the most unscrupulous methods? In the Third
Carthaginian War the Romans utterly destroyed Carthage by killing all the
men, selling all the women and children into slavery, and burning the city
to the ground. The result was that they never had any more trouble with
Carthage. That lesson has been repeated over and over well into the
contemporary world. The war conducted by the Turks in their effort to
destroy the Armenians included unspeakable atrocities. Humanitarian
methods of controlling populations are introduced only when conquering
nations feel no longer threatened.

All those who have carefully assessed the costs of wars in human lives
and suffering and artifacts destroyed, are convinced that they were not
worth waging. Wright, Angell, and many other authorities have successfully demonstrated that wars do not pay; but that does not tell anyone

how to avoid them. Moreover, the assessment may be wrong. World War 2 was certainly costly in both lives and material, but a victory by Hitler over all the Allies might have been even more costly because life for all those who would have been living under the authority of the Third Reich would have been unbearable.[6] It might be the same if the Russians are successful in their efforts to achieve world domination.

No one can predict the future of social events because there are too many variables. A few significant developments, however, should tell us something. Radical changes in warfare have been effected by the increase in the kinds of weapons deployed since the revolution in modern physics at the beginning of the 20th century, but even before that the size of standing armies had increased considerably.

It is significant that technology rather than military preparedness or personal bravery will make the difference between winners and losers -- if there are any winners! The new weapons make the whole question of man-power almost irrelevant. The neutron bomb cancels the effectiveness of those thousands of tanks the Russians have deployed, and perhaps the hydrogen bomb renders unnecessary all standing armies. It is more likely that the next war will be fought between civilian populations. The threat to the United States and the Soviet Union will come from intercontinental ballistic missles, and could be felt most between people in the geographic centers of both nations.

War has become a luxury no country can afford. Its virtues in the reduction of the aggressive need of individuals, inherited from early hunting cultures, exist no more. Other methods of need-reduction, so far as these continue to exist due to the inhertied nature of man, will have to be sought.

One final question. How can man, that most intelligent of all animals, hope to control his own destiny when he can neither understand it nor predict it? Wars before settled civilizations were only one kind of disaster, and probably not as devastating as others: floods, famines, epidemics, hurricanes, tornadoes. These are still with us, but they are on a much smaller scale than the wars which occur now periodically.

Despite major shifts in culture, however, there remains that one constant: war. People always find occasions or pretexts to fight; the reasons shift but the wars go on, and one reason seems to do as well as another. The ignorance of history, which is pretty general, has helped to generate conflicts; because it means that few have ever contemplated war's destructiveness and futility. It is difficult to tell in the middle of a campaign when there is no knowledge of precedents whether a destructive rage was the motive or the simple desire to get rid of a threat to security once and for all.

War is very nearly a constant in human history, large wars alternating with series of little wars. The fact that many occur so far away make it seem that peace rather than war is the constant, but a little reflection will disprove that. Between the two world wars and since the second, armed conflicts have been the rule rather than the exception. It is only during wars that people long for peace; during periods of peace they prepare for war. If wars often seem to lead to peace, it is because people are too exhausted and depleted to fight any longer, and so peace seems a welcome alternative. Peace at any price —— until the price seems too high and wars are fought once again.

It has taken the world a long time to recognize this fact. Rules respecting the conduct of war, intended to ameliorate the harshness and ferocity of its conditions and to humanize it —— as though peace were human and war not —— were suggested by Francis Lieber as early as 1863 but were not established until the turn of the century. The Articles of the Geneva Constitution of 1906, which resulted from the Geneva Conference of 1864, were revived at the Hague Peace Conference of 1907 as Convention X. The intentions may have been of the best but the assumptions behind such agreements have never been made plain, and what they indicate is not so favorable as might at first glance appear. The adoption of guidelines for fair play in war regularizes and legitimatizes it in a way which is hardly consistent with good international relations.

The Geneva Conventions assumed that war is here to stay and might as well be moderated. There was no thought that war could be or even should be abolished, and that is one serious objection to any agreement concerning how it should be fought. The ruthlessness and the brutality of small wars that continue to be waged around the world do not give much comfort to those who looked to the Geneva Conventions of 1864, 1906, 1929 and 1949, behind which lay the terrifying assumption that wars had to be regulated because they could not be prevented, only served to make these repeated declarations of humane treatment appear more like vain hopes than firm facts.

There have been many attempts in human history to control war. If it could not be prevented then perhaps it could be brought within the purview of order and law by being tamed. Every convening of nations, usually occurring in the wake of some tremendous conflict, has had on its agenda the making of laws respecting what would and what would not be permitted. Formal declarations of war, the treatment of prisoners, restrictions as to the type of weapons, all have been considered and even on occasion agreed to. The Charter of the League of Nations established after world war 1 and the Charter of the United Nations after world war 2 were both attempts in this direction, and both failed. When nations wish to abrogate treaties, they do so, for the morality demanded of individuals is much stricter than what is demanded of nations. The reason is simple: there is no international organization to compel compliance.

The establishment and forceful maintenance of law by legally constituted authorities within any country is a pre-condition for peace. At the present time, however, there is no accepted international law nor any legally constituted authority to see that it is enforced. Until there is, there can be no peace on any firm foundation. Peace is inseparable from law.

The highest social ambition of mankind thus far is the establishment of international law. It would enjoy a sovereignty governing all nation-states and thus would have to include all their aims short of total domination, which it would reserve for itself. International law would be the law of a world government. It assumes the existence of a social order and the imposition of justice. How this goal could be achieved short of its assumption by all is the problem. It is without a current solution; but if one is not found, we may all either perish or end as slaves.

If law is defined as an established regulation which applies equally throughout a society and is backed by force, the only hope for peace is the establishment of international law which applies equally throughout the globe and is backed —— but by what force? By definition there can be no force outside a global society, therefore none to enforce international laws. This would seem to compel a society of this dimension to be self-regulating, an arrangement which is fragile at best and probably temporary.

The only conclusion must be that if war is to be eliminated, it must be by other means. It cannot be regulated out of existence by international law. Andreski argues that the remedy against war by instituting a world government would only mean the outbreak of civil wars which could be just as bad as interstate wars or worse.[7]

The decisions to fight wars are made on the basis of local exigencies and immediate needs. Events have a way of shaping themselves, and leaders often take the credit for choices of actions they were pushed into making. With rare exceptions men of action are not men of thought. Political leaders are very good at starting wars but no good at ending them. Those responsible can never predict the outcome, which is almost always different from what had been anticipated. War leaders, even the most intelligent, like Napoleon, always count on winning, so that when they lose they are unable to cope with the situation.

Great wars are nothing less than social upheavals which end one epoch and start another. The larger the war, the greater the resulting social change. Who could have predicted conditions in the United States after the Civil War? It has been almost like two different countries, one before and one after.

Long periods of learning that are superimposed on biological needs only serve strategy, they do not eliminate conflict. Moreover, cooperative behavior is used in war as well as in peace: men unite sometimes because in this way they can intensify aggressive behavior. Mechanized warfare may come down to a matter of pressing buttons and pulling switches, but that kind of substitute for vigorous muscular force does not lessen the intense feelings of animosity that motivate individuals or satisfy their destructive needs.

Civilizations are peacetime constructions of collections of artifacts made possible by the development of superior skills. They are not the achievements of wars, which destroy them. A high level of culture is the result of the efforts of those engaged in producing works of art, scientific discoveries and precision tools. War may be said to be the very antithesis of civilization, yet its continuance is part of an ambivalent motivation, since the same people who are responsible for high civilizations also destroy them; mankind so to speak defeating itself.

Notes

1 (Chicago 1964, University of Chicago Press), 2 vols.
2 P. Sorokin, Social and Cultural Dynamics (Boston 1957, Porter Sargent).
3 Op. cit., p. 7.
4 Op. cit., p. 114.
5 Stanislav Andreski, "Origins of War" in J. D. Carthy and F. J. Ebling, The Natural History of Aggression (London 1964, Academia Press), pp. 129-130.
6 Studs Terkel, The Good War: An Oral History of World War 2 (New York 1984, Ballantine).
7 Op. cit., p. 131.

Chapter 5

THE WARRIORS 2

How difficult it is to face the fact that wars are expressions of one of the human needs! The reasons usually given for wars only describe the general behavior, not the essence. Wars are fought primarily because they are need-reducing. Judged by deeds rather than by protestations, one would have to conclude that men need wars. They certainly do behave as though this were true. Western Europe could have continued to dominate the world in peaceful fashion if it had not felt that a series of internecine conflicts was necessary, and so destroyed its own power in two world wars.

To achieve a lasting peace would require changing our nature. The 'humanist', the pacifist, the man of good will, does not have all things his own way, for he goes against the atavistic killer impulses that are still with us in strength, however submerged they may be at times.

Peace may be defined as the absence of armed conflict, but of course there is much more to it than that. Those who have opted for peace have always thought it was a matter of deliberate choice. King Henry IV and Sully in 1608 seem to have so considered it. Jean Jacques Rousseau had a high opinion of the Abbé Saint-Pierre's project for perpetual peace (1713) based on his previous work. All those involved thought the issue could be decided on psychological grounds.

The theme of Kant's essay "Toward Perpetual Peace" was suggested to him by the events of the French Revolution of 1789. He supposed that if all nations could become republics, they would engage only in rational actions, not in armed conflicts.

It was a dream that many have had who have contemplating the wreckage of wars and sought to prevent them in the future. But Kant, like the others, was planning to put a strain on human nature it would not support, for he overlooked the irrefrangible innate aggressiveness of the hunter's heritage.

Unfortunately, the traditional posture of the state has been and still is warlike. Peace is only a war that nobody wins, and before war can be eliminated altogether, peace will have to be otherwise constituted, for it has been at once the product of a common set of positive beliefs and an attitude of vigilance against a common enemy. It is easy to see how the first could be world-wide but not the second. If peace is only an organization of security, an extra-terrestrial enemy is clearly needed. If one did not exist, it would have to be invented. Any positive set of beliefs must include an established morality, but that is an internal affair. There are also external positions and actions required to protect it, and these count on continual vigilance.

There seems, too, to be a pattern to social life in which war alternates with peace, and in which one is as necessary as the other. If there does exist in fact a definite rhythm to the exercise of extreme aggression, no one seems to know its causes or periodicity. No doubt every sample population has its statistical curve, with those who are peacefully inclined at one end and those who are inherently belligerent at the other. The military draft at the outset of world war 2 was marked by as many malingerers who pretended ill health to avoid service as those who hid ailments in order to join the armed forces; cowards were as common as patriots.

The periodic alternation of peace and war seems to be imposed on man by his very nature, and there is little that he can do to escape from the dilemma. We know now that if the choice were peace or nothing, <u>he would not be equipped by nature for a permanent peace</u>. That is the essence of the problem.

All of these arguments seem to tend toward the same conclusion, namely that war has an important place in human behavior, one which is as ordinary as peace. The elimination of war as a method of settling differences seems quite out of the question, no matter how desirable it may be, because it overlooks one essential element in the nature of mankind. The unwillingness to accept such a conclusion does nothing to help us to arrive at the pacific goal at which its adherents aim.

In the late 19th and early 20th centuries there appeared in Europe and America the misleading assumption that finally men had come to their senses and would no longer appeal to war to settle their differences. Armed conflicts were to be replaced by the conference table, and differences were to be resolved at last not by fighting but by talking. International law sponsored by the League of Nations and later by the United Nations was to reign supreme, supported by all those countries who were signatories. The goodness inherent in human nature would at last prevail.

In 1910 there appeared a book entitled <u>The Great Illusion</u>. In it Norman Angell explained that another war was impossible because it had come to be regarded as unprofitable to both sides, and that no nation would be so foolish as to start one. The book was translated into many languages and had an immense sale because it proclaimed what everyone wanted to believe. A mere four years later saw the outbreak of world war 1. There were 8,000,000 combat losses before it was over, and, twenty years after that, 10,000,000 combat losses in world war 2,[1] to say nothing of the deaths in innumerable smaller wars since.

Perhaps the reason for such a misconception is that few have ever understood the nature of peace. The need for war is on exhibition all the time, for peace is the absence of conflict only of the armed variety. It is necessary to recognize that politicians do not make conflicts, they only make wars, and wars are only the intensification of conflicts. Conflicts exist already in the fact of competition. In time of peace there are conflicts at many levels: economic as well as political. Men are in competition with each other for jobs, preferment, women, prestige and many other prizes, in a condition which it would be supererogatory to describe as one of peace. What we have grown accustomed to calling peace is a confusion of conflicts which do not break out into armed violence. Then too there have been many intermediate varieties of ritualized behavior which could not be described clearly as peace or war; witness the struggles between feudal states under the Chou dynasty in ancient China when battle was a formal procedure involving the winning or losing of prestige but in which few if any on either side were killed.

Much goes on that does not deserve the name of peace.

The period between world wars is usually so described. It was nothing of the sort. The end of world war 1 in 1919 officially marked the end of conflict, but just the opposite was the case. "Peace" consisted in a long period of small wars, pogroms, race riots. It was a period of intense nationalism, with every nation bent on destroying neighbors who were traditional enemies.

The protest against an existing order is usually made on individual and social grounds in a sporadic and often politically unimportant way. It is the seed for what can become, in a later and more organized fashion, the political phenomenon of war. The elements of war are present in peace, and we shall have to make an effort to understand both if we are to learn how to abolish the former and preserve the latter.

Humanism as it was understood in the nineteenth century was a description of the good side of human nature. Man as such was identified with the man of good will, the reasonable man who means his fellow men well. Anyone who quarreled with this description of humanism, according to humanism itself, was obviously against it; and what was perfect stood in no need of improvement. Therefore, not negative criticism but satisfied complacency was the result.

Because the half-truth of this description of humanism allowed a half-falsity to survive unexamined, its results went unchecked. The favorable image of human nature has been so popular that it has blocked the way of progress. No doubt the good side does exist, but it is not the whole story. For there is, as we have noted in an earlier chapter, a bad and a negative side also, a side in which the destructive emotions come to represent all the emotions, in which prejudices take the place of reason, and in which fallacies are assumed to be the equivalent of rationality.

In particular the rationality which humanism both described and endorsed was misleading. Reason in the nineteenth century suffered from its identification with the humanistic doctrine that man is essentially good. He was good, therefore at bottom he was also rational; it was only necessary in time of threat to appeal to his reason. There are several errors here which we shall want to examine in order to get at the truths they conceal.

Ever since the Greeks it has been supposed that the rational is that of which we approve. We do not approve of the use of force, therefore force is not rational. We do not approve of the emotions, therefore emotions are not rational. And of course we do not approve of war, therefore war is not rational. The politics of rationalism of the older vintage would banish violence and conflict as irrational. But these things exist in social life and are not exceptional; therefore reason is not reason if it refuses to reckon with them.

Reason has been tested for its consistency, not for its completeness. It has to reckon with what exists and not merely with what men of good will approve. A good argument would be one that succeeded in accounting for or explaining all of the relevant facts. Too narrowly conceived, reason itself proves irrational. We have identified reason with a particular set of reasons, and the result is that some of the behavior of men has seemed entirely unreasonable. But the recognition of the ugly truths does not imply their acceptance. To say "some men enjoy war" is not the same as saying "I approve of war".

Nothing, perhaps, is more conducive to war than not providing in time of peace for all the elements which threaten it. For it is then that the forces conducive to war quietly build up. Wars are, indeed, assured when violence is left unchecked. We must begin, then, by undertaking to explain it.

We have already noted how the state takes over that portion of the aggressiveness of the individual that he cannot hope to reduce by means of his own limited powers: the drive to dominate was handed over to the state. War, then, would be simply the attempt on the part of the state to fulfill this undertaking. By means of the political instrument of the state, man endeavors to conquer his environment, and there is some satisfaction to begin with in the domination of weaker nations.

Another factor involves hunting. There is nothing new or startling in the statement that even civilized man loves to hunt. What we forget is that all sports are pursued for their enjoyment, and hunting has long been listed as a sport.

To understand it better, one has only to remember the danger involved in many other sports. The most enjoyable kind is he hunting of wild animals which threaten the hunter, such as lions, tigers, and boar. And an even more dangerous kind is the hunting of animals which at the same time are hunting the hunter. In this sense, war is a kind of hunting, the most dangerous and also the most exciting form of sport. It legalizes the aggression which is otherwise illegal, and sanctions the killing of men as a contribution to patriotism.

One explanation of the frequency of wars, then, is based on the aggressive nature of man which he inherited from hunting. In order to reduce his organic needs due to the enormous increase in human population since the early hunting cultures, the individual now requires the cooperation of his fellows. But such a social life would be impossible for an aggregation of individuals bent on mutual destruction, as would happen without any checks and balances. Hence if their aggression cannot be stopped, it must be directed outward toward a common enemy.

It comes to this, then: given the aggression of individuals expressed as a disposition to violent destruction, a viable society is possible only when an internal harmony is fostered by an external enemy. Wars seem to be necessary if there are to be peaceful societies.

The one thing that becomes clear is that there has been no progress in motivation since Neanderthal days. The ambivalence of motivation is with us still. Man still wants to help and hurt his fellows, though in both directions his methods are more refined than they were. He started, as we noted in an earlier chapter, with the shaman on the one hand and the bow and arrow on the other. But so far as methods are concerned he has progressed greatly since then, for now he has hospitals and nuclear missles.

The lust for killing other members of the same species that character- ized our most remote ancestors still characterizes us. Wars are by no means "a thing of the past", as the recent wars testify. And their ferocity has not been abated, if the massacres in Indonesia in suppressing the communist coup of 1965, or the slaughter in the civil war in Nigeria in 1967, is taken as evidence. On March 8, 1968 according to The New York Times, the International Commission of Jurists said from Geneva that if the "escalation of brutality" in Vietnam were not stopped the world might soon be emerged in a "cataclysm of horror". In 1966 the U. S. Defense Department counted 164 internationally significant outbreaks of violence in the preceding eight years, and in 1968 Carl and Shelley Mydans reported that since the end of world war 2 there had been "50 warlike conflicts of major proportions".[2]

There are more wars in progress right now than ever before. It is necessary to cite only a few to make the point: the four-year war the Russians are continuing to fight in Afghanistan, the equally old war between Iraq and Iran, the many-sided struggle between Christian and Moslem, between Moslem and Moslem and between Moslem and Israeli in the Lebanon; the inter- mittment armed struggle between Sikh and Hindu in India; the continuing war between Vietnam and Cambodia; and, more sporadic but just as fierce, the armed struggle between Roman Catholic and Protestant in northern Ireland. This by no means exhausts the lists of current conflicts but it will serve to demonstrate the prevalence.

Moreover, there is the evidence of literature to remind us that this has long been the case. The most substantial and sustained literary efforts are the folk epics. From the Sumerian epic of Gilgamesh in the third millenium BC and the epics of Homer, to the Alexander Romance in the Middle Ages in Europe, the treasured writings of all peoples have been concerned with wars. There is no other literature capable of matching the epics in scope and intensity, and there is no other with the same degree of popularity. People love to hear tales of battles and the heroes who fought in them.

Many of the great civilizations only become great after doing battle with their neighbors. In the most important civilizations war was thought to be as natural as peace. In ancient China and India battles were fought with large numbers of men, and it was so in ancient Greece where the citizen was always a potential warrior. In the Islamic world religion was tightly wrapped up with fighting. The Germans and the Japanese before and during world war 2 —— though certainly not afterwards —— glorified war as the highest destiny of man. No human history would possibly be written without an account of the wars which punctuate the periods of peace with a revealing regularity. The inclination toward war exists in all those countries which consider themselves powerful enough to wage it, and as Morgenthau has pointed out, both victory and defeat in war give rise to the same imperialistic policies.[3]

But political unities exist as much for negative as for positive reasons, and people make common cause as often because they fear a common enemy as because they see positive gains in working together. Just as often the negative presents itself as positive. The brief-lived OAU, the Organization of African Unity of the 1970s, and OPEC, the Organization of

Petroleum Exporting Countries, are good examples.

It can be argued, for instance, that the range of weapons determines the size of the state. Artillery destroyed the antiquated castle of the feudal lord and replaced it with the nation-state on a small scale. The emergence of a complex economy made possible the existence of a professional army which could be based permanently on the frontiers, thus making possible a peace within geographical boundaries. But when the first military airplanes flew over national borders in Europe in world war 1, the fate of the small modern nation was sealed, and only large international coalitions could hope to survive. Finally, with the development of the nuclear arsenal, a global government became imperative.

It seems to go against human interest to venerate human destruction, yet the politicians who are best remembered and most highly regarded are the war lords, those leaders who succeeded in getting the greatest number of people killed: Alexander, Genghis Khan, Timurlane, Caesar, Napoleon, Lincoln, Roosevelt. The leaders do not lead in such cases, they only follow deep instincts which are imbedded in the genes of every human individual. The more power the politicians have, the more such instincts find their logical social outlet. The need for war arises in the individual as one of his inherited nature, and finds its expression in leaders who are leaders because of their usefulness to this side.

So long as decisions concerning war and peace are in the hands of politicians, it is only necessary to remember that the use of thermonuclear weapons and the control of the mass media give the contemporary political leader the power to preserve life or deal death for millions and perhaps for the entire human species. It is more power than he ever had before and more than anyone should have now. Technological advances drive social developments further and faster, but always in the direction in which they were heading.

There exist social reservoirs of power of which we have been unaware and for which we must find an outlet at regular periods. The effect of abolishing wars might have its own disastrous consequences because of the energy which fails to be released. With our lack of requisite knowledge of social psychology, it is difficult at this stage to be sure. Although war fills with horror those who have any hope for humanity on its constructive side, the evidence is not all clear that everyone shares this view. World sympathy is extended to the victims of aggression only when the aggression is long and protracted. No one seems to have evinced much interest in the Baltic states when the Soviet Union absorbed them. There was nowhere as much sympathy for South Korea as there was for South Vietnam. Sympathy needs time to develop, and a quick conquest does not allow for it.

Things that are not good politics are worse for humanity the more efficiently they are done. Were it not for the inept military mind, mankind would long ago have vanished. It may be taken as axiomatic that the human condition is arduous enough; life is short and filled with pain and difficulties, to say nothing of natural human enemies which always abound, such as predatory animals and hostile climates, without adding the woes of torturing, fighting, wounding, and killing. Intra-specific aggression does seem to be peculiar to humanity.

Hegel argued that Kant's "perpetual peace" would be stagnating and that war is healthy. Also, he said, war abroad insures peace at home. As to the point that peace is stagnating, we do not have the experience and so cannot tell, for we have never had peace long enough to be able to watch its prolonged effects. As to the point that war is healthy, well, Hegel always

predicted his political theories upon the certainty of German victories. I
am not sure that even Hegel would have been able to regard the destruction
of Dresden and Hamburg, and the defeat of Germany and its consequent
reduction to a second class power in world war 2, as healthy.

The difficulty with the appeal to war is that no one can tell who will
be the victor. Also, it often happens that the so-called victor proves to
be the loser and the loser, the victor. Japan, the loser, has done better
in economic terms since world war 2 than England, the victor. The outcome
of a war is almost never the same as the predictions about it.

Hegel's final point, that war abroad insures peace at home, is a telling
one and has frequently been resorted to by dictators who felt their hold
slipping or who encountered problems they knew could not be solved. Nothing
brings the people of a country so close together and rallies them under the
flag no matter how serious their other difficulties as a common enemy. The
French Resistance of world war 2 united communists, Roman Catholic priests,
and politicians of all stripes in a common cause because they were all
Frenchmen and wanted the Germans driven out.

The difficulty with Hegel's argument is that war abroad is easy to start
and sometimes difficult to stop. Then, too, sometimes it is lost and the
war abroad suddenly appears in the form of invading troops which makes things
even more uncomfortable and less than peaceful. The Germans who invaded
Russia found this out before they were done.

It is a curious arrangement when, in return for the privilege of
participating in civil order, the state can exact the life of its citizens.
This remains, true, certainly, so long as there is a military draft; and it
is true for the citizens whether all of them like it or not. Death is a
high price to pay for an orderly life, and that is what it comes down to,

at least for those who die for their country; and this remains true whether
or not they have chosen to do so. In any case, the outcome lies in the
social domain. For just as the stability of the individual rests on an
equilibrium between competing needs and drives, so peace within the state as
well as between nations is a matter of balance between conflicting interests
and opposing coalitions. All such arrangements — individual, federal,
international — are uneasy affairs, but then so are all social systems.

As we approach the close of the twentieth century, we can see that it
has been worse than many previous centuries in the size and frequency of its
wars. There is nothing in the present picture or the prospects for the
immediate future that might encourage us to think that this will change.
In addition to wars there are many other kinds of violent aggression, and
in the following chapters we shall have a look at some of the more
prevalent.

Notes

1 L. I. Dublin and M. Spiegelman, The Facts of Life (New York 1951,
Macmillan), p. 406.
2 Carl Mydans and Shelley Mydans, The Violent Peace (New York 1968,
Atheneum).
3 Hans J. Morgenthau, Politics among Nations (New York 1967, Knopf),
pp. 3676.

Chapter 6

THE BELIEVERS

Everyone these days knows intuitively what is meant by belief, though definitions are not that common. A belief is the feeling that a proposition is true.[1] In that meaning of the word, we are all believers; in certain cases, however, much more is involved: there is for instance absolute belief, which is the feeling that a proposition is true beyond the possibility of a doubt. That is the version I propose to examine here.

Let me first, though, clear up one source of confusion by distinguishing between absolute belief and the belief in absolutes. The belief in absolutes does not itself have to be absolute. It is possible to say, "I am considering this absolute proposition, but thus far I do not accept it absolutely." I mean to discuss here only the belief of those who do accept it absolutely, which often means, incidentally, holding a belief long after the memory of the grounds on which it was originally accepted have faded. Absolute belief here means absolute acceptance.

1

Although the commonest of all absolute beliefs are of course the religious beliefs, there are others: the belief in the white race, in astrology, or in the absolute truth of Marxism, for instance. What is not so well known perhaps is that, as Napoleon said, "the ambition to dominate men's minds is the strongest of all the passions".[2] Unfortunately, the majority of individuals have no mental independence and so look for someone to exercise this kind of control over them.

What is not so well known is that there are degrees of absolute belief, because the term 'absolute' implies an exclusive commitment; whereas there are in fact three kinds of commitment, ranged according to the strength of their effects, which can be either simple, obsessive, or compulsive, corresponding to the three capacities of the human individual, which are for (a) feeling, (b) thought and (c) action, respectively.

(a) Absolute belief is always at least a _feeling_. Because it is absolute, the feeling is one of total conviction, a complete surrender to a point of view which yields a feeling of security. This kind of absolute believer may undergo a spiritual conversion, as when he finds himself committed to a new set of beliefs; and these may affect all his evaluations. The commonest form of absolute belief is the religious variety. An absolute believer in a traditional religion regards anyone who holds the same firm attitude but not to _his_ religion as a "fanatic", by which is meant a believer in some _other_ religion.

Konrad Lorenz has well described the feeling of absolute belief. He calls it a "powerful phylogentically evolved behavior" involving "militant enthusiasm".[3] It is, he claims, "a true autonomous instinct with its own releasing mechanisms, its own appetitive behavior, and it engenders a feeling of intense satisfaction".[4] There is no greater social force than a system of ideas at the metaphysical level of abstraction which is identified with the name of a particular individual, such as Buddha,

Confucius, Moses, Jesus, Mohammed, or Marx.

Truth, alas, has nothing to do with it. As it happens, "human aggression is never more terrifying than when at the service of the dogmatic and delusory group of ideologies.....For abstractions men will die like flies and exterminate each other with every instrument of destruction and no less when they are false".[5]

Nobody has ever given sufficient credit to the role of the feelings in sustaining and confirming false beliefs. The degree of conviction in their case is actually stronger because their simplicity makes them easier to grasp and hence to defend. The absolute believer may not believe in much, but he invokes strong passions in support of what he does believe.

(b) In addition to feeling, absolute belief may be also a matter of thought. In that case the absolute believer simply cannot think of anything else; his beliefs and their consequences become obsessive and occupy his entire available time. In this category are often to be found the most intelligent individuals. They use their ability to deal with abstractions in order to reinforce their beliefs by means of tradition and by rational speculation, with the feelings turned toward the acceptance of premises and deductions from them. The absolute believer of this sort may also become a professional religious, or as a laymen seek converts. He will understand everything, however unrelated, in this new light.

Unfortunately, absolute belief often has the support of ignorance, which as it happens is not the mere absence of knowledge but the presence of false knowledge, the firm belief in what is not so. No head is empty but many are filled with falsities of all sorts, false 'facts' as well as false theories. It is a characteristic of many individuals lacking intelligence that to them belief comes easily.

The absolute believer has a kind of active intolerance. No two sets of absolute beliefs can live peacefully in the world together, for every expression of a rival absolute belief provokes a violent reaction. The comfort of absolute belief makes it a foe of reason because difficult to reject emotionally. It does not allow access to the counter-evidence but in fact is closed off. There is in short a closure-deafness to much of speculative thought.

Finally, (c) absolute belief may take the form of <u>action</u>. The absolute believer of this kind carries his compulsion into practice. Given the strength of his belief, he is ready to engage in violent activity, such as the murder of a non-believer. The <u>kamikaze</u> Japanese pilots who in world war 2 flew their planes into American warships, and the Muslim fundamentalists who in 1984 in the Lebanon drove a truck loaded with dynamite into the American Marine compound, are good examples of absolute believers in action. So are the terrorists, the torturers, and the revolutionaries who do not hesitate to kill not only men but also women and children out of a total conviction in the fundamental rightness of their cause.

Perhaps the most extreme current example of absolute belief is that of the Iranian leader, the Ayatollah Khomeini, who in a public address concerning the continuance of the war with Iraq was quoted as saying that Islam had made the Iranian people godly to the extent that they are now dressing their children in burial shrouds and saying they want to send them to be martyred. "This is unprecedented in the history of man", he added. [6]

Absolute belief is qualitatively different from other kinds of belief. They may be harmless; it is not. Many a gentle individual leading a softly cultured life under tranquil circumstances would be surprised to learn how very violent and destructive the logical consequences of his privately-held absolute beliefs would be if he or she acted on them.

People are transformed by absolute belief. They are no longer the sane and rational creatures they once were, though outward conformity makes them seem so. Instead the roles are reversed, and they become the instruments of their belief, losing sympathy with all those who lie outside their circle. They are not aware that they have come to regard their belief as an end and themselves as its means. They have turned into the obedient servants of an abstraction and forgot the meaning of all their contacts with the concrete. If the world around them does not conform to their beliefs in every respect, well then, it must be made to.

Thus the absolute believer is always a crusader, who would kill you if you persist in refusing to accept his beliefs —— and moreover he would do it for your own good! Thus there is room in any given society for only one set of absolute beliefs. When there is more than one, there is usually an armed struggle, ending with the defeat and death of the losers.

Absolute belief of whatever variety must be regarded as the greatest enemy of the human species because of its destructive nature, this is true not only of its effects on others but also on the believer himself. It eventually comes to rest deep in the subconscious mind, so deep that it cannot be reached, and this makes it invulnerable.

Built into the succession of the generations, it comes naturally to those born into a society long established. Remember that the child is by nature an authority-acceptor. He is provided with a faith by his parents, his teachers, the community, when he is young and most impressionable. It would be difficult not to be a believing Hindu in Bombay or Madras or a believing Moslem in Tehran or Isfahan.

Absolute belief has the added property that it tends to spread. This gives it an awesome force. All beliefs, therefore, should carry a warning label reading "Contagious When Absolute". The reason for its strength is the comfort which accompanies every absolute belief. The absolute believer, be he Christian, Moslem, Jewish, Hindu, Buddhist or Marxist, is convinced that the good feeling which accompanies every absolute believer is a feature only of that particular belief.

This is emphatically not the case, however. All faiths are comforting and all are equally so. What could be a more telling argument against faith as a form of belief? Given that the most absurd beliefs have been found to serve just as well as the more reasonable, it follows that the reassurance that comes from absolute belief is no valid argument in favor of its truth.

The last justification, then, for the holding of an absolute belief is the assurance it gives the believer. An absolute belief is much easier to live with than a state of doubt. Doubt is uncomfortable; the doubter does not dare to act because of his uneasy state of uncertainty and his feeling of insecurity. The search for truth and consequently for acceptable beliefs involves a suspension of judgment which cannot be sustained for very long. The painful condition of doubt is the price which must be paid for the freedom to discover truths. It is doubt that makes possible the consideration of alternatives and the choice of the best one, but it requires both greater strength of character and considerably more intelligence to doubt than to believe.

The absolute believer, then, is not open to objections to his convictions. If he were he would have to consider the untenability of his position. There is strong evidence against all absolute belief, one which may be summarized in a single statement;

Absolute belief is one kind of absolute but there are no absolutes of
any kind in the material world.

The argument rests on the assumption that there are two distinctly
different kinds of being: a world of material things and a closely related
domain of abstract ideas. The former is the ordinary world that we live in,
and it consists in particulars of matter and energy. The other, somewhat
separate, contains the universals of logic and mathematics. The world of
material things is also one of events; it is where things happen. By
contrast, nothing ever 'happens' in logic, which is a set of abstract
relationships that never changes but can be traversed over and over again
by calculating.

All perfection belong to logic. The reason why there can be no absolutes
in the material world is because everything there is limited. Thus in order
to make the laws of the physical sciences apply to that world, though they
are framed in absolute terms, it is always necessary to add a provision.
The law of gravitation, which accounts for the mutual attraction of all
material bodies according to a fixed rate, is stated for a vacuum, and the
degree of interference (of air, etc.) has to be added to every particular
calculation.

How does this distinction apply to a claim to the possession of the
absolute truth? It means that the 'truth' of any absolute truth belongs
to the domain of logic, so that when an absolute truth is employed in the
world of matter, it must be qualified. If a believer wishes to act on
some truth which he accepts, then, he must remember to modify it in
practice according to the extenuating circumstances.

In short, the absolutist is behaving in the fallible and limited
material world in accordance with his beliefs even though these apply

66

absolutely only in the domain of logic. Small wonder, then, that the effects of his thoughts, feelings and actions are destructive: they are out of place. The true believer must be content with more modest claims.

2

So much for the positive effects of absolute belief. Now let us look at the negative effects. These may be called absolute disbeliefs, and they are much greater. For it happens that every absolute believer has to be also an absolute disbeliever. That is to say, he disbelieves strongly in all absolute beliefs that conflict with his own. If, for instance, he is an absolute believer in a particular established religion, then it follows that he is also an absolute disbeliever in all of the others. Hence statistically his disbeliefs must out-weigh his beliefs by some very large amount.

Any absolute disbelief, by itself, then, and without any deliberate implication must be responsible for the enmity and opposition to all other such beliefs, and, because it is absolute, takes overt and violent forms. In a word, any absolute belief which by inference excludes all others is in its posture aggressive and in its actions challenging, and so always reasy for open conflict. Absolute disbelief as an immediate and direct consequence of absolute belief may have more serious consequences because it rarely tarries at thoughts and feelings but is carried as quickly as possible into action in the social arena.

That those who hold to absolute disbeliefs always do violence to others is amply illustrated by the history of Christianity in modern times. In the 16th century "wars of religion" in Europe, the Roman Catholic Church sought to repress the rising movement of Protestantism. The violence of that struggle is a matter of record; massacres were quite common in which women and children were killed.

Wars of religion and wars of conquest furnish historically the most dramatic examples, and they are still with us, and in our own day have been added the wars of the Marxists to destroy the political systems of others, carried out in terms of absolute destruction to match the absoluteness of beliefs. There was for instance the persecution of the Buddhists in Tibet by the Communist Chinese, of Christians and Jews in Cuba and the Soviet Union, also the persecution of Jehovah's Witnesses in South Africa and of the Baha'i in Iran.[7]

Unfortunately, other examples of genocide prompted by absolute disbelief are not hard to come by in the modern world. It is possible to cite Hitler's extermination of the Jews, Pol Pot's massacre of his own people in Cambodia, and currently the Shi'ite Moslem war against the Christian Palestinians, as well as the armed struggle between Protestant and Roman Catholic in northern Ireland and between Sikh and Hindu in northern India (1985).

In every country in recent decades there have been isolated revolution- ary groups intent on destruction. They have taken different names, like the Weathermen in Chicago, and they have bombed indiscriminately, regarding as their enemy any beneficiaries of the established order. They have not spared women and children, for their bombs have been planted in public squares, shopping centers, even in ordinary streets, in fact anywhere people were expected to gather. In the Lebanon at the present time they are particularly in evidence. The various doctrines to which they give adherence has no common source; they might be Marxists, revolutionaries of the left, Islamic fundamentalists, or some other. They have in common only that they are all equally absolutists.

The advocates of democracy have had a mistaken conviction that an individual's beliefs are his own and that no one has a right to interfere with them or to dictate changes. This is true in so far as it applies to moderate beliefs but wholly untrue if they are absolute; for from their adherents we may eventually expect a destructive onslaught intended to bring us into conformity. There is, then, literally all the difference in the world between the effects of a moderate disbelief and those of an absolute disbelief, and we need to recognize that difference before it puts us in peril.

3

One important variety of negative absolute belief (or absolute disbelief) is called nihilism. Nihilism arose as a Russian variety of revolutionary anarchism. The term was given authority by Turgeniev's use of it in his novel Fathers and Children first published in 1862. It was a product of the Russian revolutionary philosophy in the late 19th century which held that nothing is valuable and hence that all established laws and institutions must be totally rejected, all existing social and political establishments abolished. Violence was the approved method for achieving this end; it included terrorism and assassination, and even massacre; in a word, total and absolute destruction.

Nihilism is as much a philosophy as any other, for it promotes in a positive way the ontological theory of nothingness. The true nihilist is an action absolutist; for him or her there are no hard facts, only inter-pretations, no history, only meanings.

One well known variety of nihilism was called anarchism. It had ancient roots but arose as a popular movement in modern times as a reaction to extreme monarchy and the rise of capitalism. Godwin's two volumes published in 1793 and Proudhon in 1840 were the theoretical apologists of the movement which found its first and greatest overt expression in the French Revolution of 1789. A society without government and life without restraints of any kind were what it advocated. Not surprisingly it gave rise to many acts of violence, especially through the labor movement. Both nihilism and anarchism, needless to add, are absolute beliefs.

There is no hope for the human species to come from any absolute belief. It always involves violence, and, worse than that: always invokes more violence in its opposite number. The extremely pious and totally observant adherent of any religious faith, however peaceful, does not comprehend that he or she is laying the groundwork for clashes of faith and wars of religion, but that nevertheless is the case. The exclusivity of absolute believers forces resentment on outsiders. Absolute belief in any one social group provokes a violent response from others, thus leaving no room for an orderly settlement of differences.

There are so far as I can discover no exceptions to this general rule. Consider for example the most pacific of absolute beliefs, those of the Hinayana Buddhist. He is an absolute believer in non-being and an absolutist in his denial of life; he rejects the idea of a soul, of consciousness, and even of a future. The community of believers is ignored, and at the same time all effort is concentrated on doing violence to the idea of a separate self. Buddhism is nihilism carried over into the next world by preparing the individual for it in this one through the slow process of self-destruction.

4

Unfortunately, absolute beliefs are quite common. Most people subscribe to them in one version or another, and those who do are always ready to put them into practice. They never think about those who are prepared to act from other absolute beliefs.

Once the posture is achieved of accepting an absolute truth, it becomes easy to exchange one absolute for another. Many of the most devoted of Roman Catholics in southern Italy had no difficulty in either exchanging it for communism or else accepting both, notwithstanding that they were and still are mutually exclusive. Having an absolute truth is a way of life affecting behavior in all of its departments, and this is not disturbed by exchanging one absolute truth for another. What is much more difficult is giving up absolute truth altogether and opting for a working belief that makes actions possible while involving the individual in no final commitments.

With sufficient social organization and the determination of leaders, whole societies can be programmed by the adoption of an absolute truth. The success of 'world' religions attest to this. Certainly it is the story of Christianity and now currently of Marxism. Belief is self-reinforcing: surrounded by absolute believers on every side, how could an individual ever succeed in doubting its truth? Only an exceptional individual who did not wish to struggle with the question of belief versus doubt in the first place. It is far easier to believe than to doubt and also far more comfortable. That leaves the result pre-determined.

The amazing thing is not that belief succeeds but that any doubt survives. That it does is a tribute to the fact that the isolation of a society from all outside information is never total. The news must creep in despite all the efforts to prevent it that there are peoples beyond the information barriers who do not accept it. The day will never come with Marxism despite its military successes that the whole world will be a self-contained shell of absolute belief in Marxism. Ignorance, of course, helps such a position, and there is a lot of it in countries practicing a fundamentalist religion, like the Muslims of Iran or the Hindus in remote Indian villages. But even such ignorance is never total and even so it is not for long.

Sometimes it happens that a belief belongs to the individual alone, and then we are dealing with psychopathology. The mentally ill individual who thinks that he is the incarnation of the avenging angel may be placed in a psychiatric hospital before he harms anyone.

But what about the many instances where the beliefs and actions are those of a social group among whose members the individual can find all the support he needs in the way of agreement and assistance and with whom he can act in concert? Far from being criminal types, they are to the contrary the norm by which criminals are judged. For example in contemporary Iran, any able-bodied young citizen who refused to take part in the killing of a member of the Baha'i faith would have to be considered disobeying the Ayatollah Khomeini, the de facto ruler of his country. The very same killer who in Tehran was judged a leading citizen would in New York be a criminal though "not guilty by reason of insanity". In the Soviet Union at the present time it is a familiar price to judge insane and send to a mental institution any citizen who tries to monitor adherence to the Helsinki Accord.[8]

If an individual can seem made in one society and quite sane in another, it is fair to ask at this point, where does madness leave off and social conformity begin? How, in short, does one distinguish between a religious zealot and a psychotic killer? Which is the conformist and which the criminally insane? This is not entirely an arbitrary question but depends upon where one takes a reading.

Under this arrangement by tacit agreement it is assumed that _my_ absolute beliefs rest on truth, _yours_ on falsehoods, and it is assumed that the many absolute beliefs that at present abound in the world have nothing in common except for the psychological fact that they _are_ beliefs.

I see no way out of this conflict, at least none that would be acceptable to all parties. The result is almost an uncountable number of ongoing conflicts, from the clash in India between Sikh and Hindu to the tribal wars to be found almost everywhere in Africa, not counting the opposition bordering on open war which have ancient roots and which the contemporary Marxists, aided and abetted by agents from the Soviet Union, are quick to exploit. Malcontents whose resentment of a system which excludes them from its benefits can find a justification for their endorsement of destructive-ness in the writings of Marx, Engels and Lenin.

5

We tend to regard as irrational what has not yet been rendered amenable to reason. That points however to the limitations of human reasoning, not to a deficiency in the laws of logic.

The relation of reason to madness has not been well understood. The madman is not necessarily irrational, he merely accepts a different set of premises. Accordingly, his actions, which seem quite irrational to _us_, for him may follow inexorably from the set _he_ accepts and thus seem quite rational to him.

Any therapy would have to include a method for getting at his premises in order to change them, a difficult assignment when you consider how deep in the mind the acceptance of premises lies and how long ago for the individual most such acceptance had occurred. The situation would be rendered even more difficult —— even hopeless, in the opinion of some —— when the same set of premises are those of a large group of religious believers whose uniform behavior would furnish all the reinforcement necessary.

A definition of madness eventually emerges from these considerations. Madness consists not in the absence of a logical system but rather in the assumption by an individual that the only admissable premises are his premises and the only conclusions those he draws from them. The madman has his own set of premises and consequent actions which follow logically but which he shares with no one.

Here perhaps we can best see why our on-going conception of human nature is in need of revision. We cannot make it up wholly of principles that we approve or out of conduct that for many good reasons we endorse. That is the lesson of madness, as Foucault has pointed out. "The madness of desire, insane murders, the most unreasonable passions —— all are wisdom and reason, since they are part of [human] nature".[9] Nothing that exists can be regarded as unnatural, and this is especially true of what recurs. Madness recurs.

Foucault was surely on to something when he set madness at the limits of reason, for the irrationality of the madman is an irrefrangible part of the picture of human nature. The individual is taken care of but not the larger aspects of society when madness became "mental illness with its own appropriate branch of medicine".[10] All societies whatever beliefs they are organized around, are always rough at the edges, always contain or exclude —— it is much the same thing —— non-conformists who are deemed criminal.

When madness spreads to the center of a nation, the result is a self-destructive society, such as Hitler's Germany. Were such a society to flourish and include the whole world, mankind would be threatened, and it might be the end of everything. Thus far, madness has proved self-limiting for it promotes its own active opposition, and this condition may be inherent in it.

It is certainly true that we cannot live in the world of the madman with him. With certain changes and adjustments, however, he can live in our world with us. Hence the importance of psychiatrists and hospitals. The madman does not project a world in which even he can live alone for very long. It has its own logical system but there are few theorems that can be deduced from its premises and carried out in practice. The differences are crucial for everyone, and fortunately there is a remedy available.

In an earlier work Foucault proposed a criterion by means of which sanity could be distinguished from madness.[11] Madness, he suggested, could be defined by the absence of material works; there are no viable constructions by the insane. Instead, man can be defined by what he makes; the world of artifacts in a sane world. It is certainly true of the revolutionary, the nihilist, the terrorist and the torturer, that he constructs nothing, only destroys.[12] That may not be much protection, but it is all that we have.

There is in a certain sense no place to go. Why is there human life? So far as an ultimate purpose is concerned, we are forever condemned to the search for an absolute answer while at the same time being forever precluded from finding one. Nothing is more damaging to the human species than the occasional claims to the discovery of the absolute truth. The

paradox of human nature is the immense following that such claims are able

to generate. It would seem that one of the more reliable constants of human

existence is the inflicting of pain and even death on those who refuse to

accept the current version.

Notes

1 For a detailed description of belief, see my Adaptive Knowing (Martinus Nijhoff, The Hague, 1976, chapter 11; also "The Nature of Belief" in Tulane Studies in Philosophy, New Orleans, La., 1981.

2 Quoted in Elie Faure, Napoleon, J. E. Jeffrey trans. (New York 1925, Alfred A. Knopf), p. 32.

3 On Aggression, M. K. Wilson trans. (New York 1963, Harcourt Brace & World), p. 268.

4 Ibid., p. 271.

5 Quoted in J. D. Carthy and F. J. Ebling, The Natural History of Aggression (London 1964, Academic Press), pp. 114.

6 A United Press International release on June 21, 1985, in the New Orleans Times-Picayune, p. A-8.

7 David A. Price, in The Wall Street Journal for June 10, 1985, p. 16.

8 Eric Stover and Elena O. Nightingale, The Breaking of Bodies and Minds (New York 1985, W. H. Freeman), Part 2.

9 Michael Foucault, Madness and Civilization (New York 1973, Random House), Conclusion.

10 Vincent Descombes, Modern French Philosophy (Cambridge 1980, Cambridge University Press), p. 115.

11 The Order of Things (New York 1971, Pantheon Books), 10, 3.

12 Bernard-Henri Lévy, Barbarism with a Human Face. George Holoch, trans. (New York 1979, Harper & Row).

Chapter 7

THE SLAVERS

The article on slavery occupies 14 large pages in the 14th edition of
the Encyclopaedia Britannica. That amount of space in double-columned
pages was required to give even the most superficial account of the practice.

Slavery may be defined as the enforced bondage of another and therefore
as compelling involuntary servitude.

The condition we find so abhorrent is in fact one of the oldest and
most time-honored institutions. Many ancient texts reveal a concern with
seeing to it that slaves are treated fairly, not with the possibility of
doing away with the practice altogether.

How old is slavery? We do not know, but a good guess is possible.
Probably as old as the distinction between the Desert and the Sown, between
the first settlements and the surrounding nomads. The shift from hunting
and gathering to metal-using societies occurred sometime from c.8000 to
c.2000 BC.[1] That produced an enmity based on the conditions of the haves
and the have-nots, the nomads raiding for the possessions of the city-
dwellers.

It must have been recognized early, then, that the two groups had more
to separate them than to unite them. The separation was a result of lack
of communication; the development of distinct languages and customs would
emphasize differences over similarities. Thus the idea that all human

beings were all equally members of a single interbreeding species would not have occurred to anyone. Its place was taken by interest and advantage, which always came from identification with a limited group.

The intermittent and almost constant series of violent conflicts between those with different associations and interest would erase any possibility of a conception of a common humanity, and in its place leave only the struggle for advantage. If one tribe was victorious over another, it would seem the logical thing to do to kill the men and enslave the women and children of the others. Female slaves in time bred with their masters, but their offspring were also slaves; and so a slave population would grow up in the midst of a victorious and free people. Thus it might happen that slavery could become a useful institution and moreover one that was regarded as quite natural. It is certainly true that from the earliest records we have, slavery was a part of the cultural scheme of things. It remained so until recent times.

Slavery evidently had its place in the earliest records. It was already recognized in the Babylonian Code of Hammurabi (about 1800 BC) and in the Assyrian laws (about 1350 BC). Slavery is clearly sanctioned in Deuteronomy 15, the Code found in the Temple in 621 BC. It was fully established as an accepted custom in the Homeric period; prisoners taken in war were sold as slaves or maintained in that capacity.[2]

In short, slavery in the world of the earliest civilizations was the rule, and it was probably without exception. The origins of slavery as an established institution will probably never be known because the records are almost wholly lost, at least so far as intimate social conditions are concerned. Civilizations first arose in river valleys: the lower Tigris and Euphrates, the Nile, the Indus and the Yellow River. Their common characteristic was the appearance of the city, with its divisions of labor, its literacy, public buildings, political and religious hierarchies, and ultimately its claim to empire. They may have all practiced slavery, but we simply do not know.

The idea that all humans share a common humanity and therefore are entitled to the rights of equality was a very recent arrival on the social scene. Indeed the inequality of the various segments of mankind was an unquestioned premise. It would be interesting to speculate on when and where and by whom the idea that all human individuals are equal with respect to a common humanity was first expressed and put into practice. Was it as late as we think it was, based on the evidence, or were early doctrines destroyed so that we have no record of them? It is difficult to say. All of history points the other way, for even the writings of the best minds of the past do not seem to have excluded slavery as a conventional institution.

It is painful but necessary to remember that ancient Greece despite all its glory was a slave-holding society, as was too the Roman Empire at its height.

In the many references to slavery scattered throughout the Dialogues of Plato, it is clear that he regarded it as an accepted practice which he had no thought of abolishing or even of disapproving. In cautioning against the abuse of the institution, he inadvertently assumed that it was here to stay.[3]

Slavery was also accepted by Aristotle as both necessary and natural. In the Ethica Eudemia he makes the comparison of the body as the soul's tool and the slave as a tool of the master.[4] In the Ethica Nichomachea he discusses the possibility of a slave's happiness.[5] The only objection was to having Greeks for slaves. Other Greek authorities, such as Epicurus approved of the practice of slavery, while the only concession of humanists like Euripides was that slaves should be treated fairly, remembering that they too were people.

In ancient Rome slavery was a well-established institution. Athenaeus, who lived in Rome in the second century AD, devoted pages of his 15-volume books of gossip, the Doctors at Dinner, to the topics of slaves, their various kinds and functions.[6] There can be little doubt after reading him of the prevalence of the institution. There were slave markets throughout the Empire where slaves imported from Africa, Spain and Gaul were sold to Roman citizens. It was a poor family indeed that did not have any, for the men worked the fields while their females served in the household. Gibbon in his history estimates the proportion of slaves to free men as three to one. In the reign of Claudius he estimated that there were some 20 million slaves, probably a fair guess.

The Greeks and Romans were no exception. In the Persian Empire slavery was taken for granted as a part of the natural arrangement of the population.

Slavery existed wherever the religion of Islam triumphed, which was over at least one seventh of the known world. To order good treatment for slaves, as the Koran does, is tacitly to recognize it as a legitimate institution. Mohammed was born in Mecca in AD 570. The religion founded in his name spread rapidly during his later years and even more after his death, and with it the custom of slavery. From the coast of the Red Sea where it started, it went on to conquer most of North Africa and much of Asia. In the 12th century Saladin added Syria and Egypt to the Muslim world. The Mongol Empire spread over northern Asia, and incorporated Islam in the

course of its conquests. That was in the 13th and 14th centuries. By the
15th century the Ottoman Empire had added Asia Minor and the northern coast
of the Black Sea from Moldavia to the Crimea. Europe was threatened a
number of times but succeeded in surviving.

In the Middle Ages, serfdom was a natural accomplishment of the agricultural economy of feudalism. Originally serfdom arose as a result of
military conquest, but it remained for economic reasons. Serfdom is usually
thought of as an intermediate condition between slavery and freedom, but
there are degrees of slavery, and it all depends upon the definition of the
term. The serf was not his own master; and, while, he was not legally
owned by the lord, he was tied to the lord's land. There were checks on the
lord's power over his serfs, but they were his, and to that extent the
condition should be classed as a kind of modified slavery.

Slavery was a feature of the Spanish colonies in the New World,
beginning with Henry the Navigator in 1442, who had pursued the practice on
the coast of Africa. The lucrative character of these transactions inspired
others to capture natives in Haiti for sale in Portugal. Columbus in 1494
sent home 500 Indian prisoners to be sold as slaves in Seville. Caribs,
Cubans and Porto Ricans received much the same treatment. Later, the flow
was reversed, and English slave traders were busy supplying African slaves
to the British colonies of America and the West Indies. 192 British slave
ships carried as many as 47,000 Africans into slavery. The Portugese in
their occupation of Angola and Mozambique copied the slavery taught them by
the Africans, and there was also a slave trade to Brazil.

African chiefs aided the business of procuring slaves for the Europeans.
They set fire to villages and captured the natives trying to escape the
flames. The loss of life in the traffic was immense. It has been

estimated that more than 12% died during the passage to the West Indies, 4½% while in harbor, and one third more while in process of being sold. They did not prosper in all of the colonies, partly from ill treatment and partly because of a large excess of males over females, but they did well in the southern United States.

The system of serfdom in old Russia continued to be little more than a name for slavery. The serfs were a recognized class and treated as such under the laws and procedure of the state. Slaves under the reign of Catherine 2 were bought and sold or given away like any other commodity.

The Spanish and Portugese slave trade continued well into the nineteenth century. Movements for the reform of these conditions did not occur until then. Jean Lafitte, the pirate of French descent who lived on an island in the Gulf of Mexico just below the city of New Orleans, was engaged in the active trading of slaves. He and his pirates raided Spanish ships filled with slaves, while his brother Pierre ran the blacksmith shop in the French Quarter of New Orleans which was a blind for the sale of slaves to the southern planters who needed them. After the end of the war of 1812, though pardoned by the Governor of Louisiana for his services to the American cause, Lafitte resumed the lucrative practice. When ships of the United States Navy were sent to apprehend him, he fled with his fleet to Campeche (modern Galveston, Texas), and had to be chased away from there, also by the Navy. He died still pursuing the slave trade on the coast of Central America.

Slavery, as everyone knows, was abolished formally in 1865, but only after a bitter four-year civil war was fought over it. That was little more than a century ago! Slavery was before that an established institution in the southern United States, where slaves worked the cotton fields and

performed other menial tasks. Household slaves were a familiar sight among
the old plantation families. Slavery continued to be practiced in many
parts of the world. Before and during world war 1, there were slaves in
Germany used in industries necessary to the war effort. Under Stalin the
concentration camps were sources of supply for the forced slave labor
employed on a large scale in the building of airports, roads, canals and
railways. Slaves were employed also in gold mines, the mining of coal,
industrial agriculture and transport. For the big Baltic-White Sea Canal,
300,000 slaves were used.[7]

In world war 2, hundreds of thousands of concentration camp inmates were
"leased out" to German industries, such as the Krupps, Messerschmidt and
Heinkel, as slave labor. In addition to this operation which was master-
minded by Himmler, he ran his own factories with the same kind of slaves.

The earliest attempts to end it were at the Berlin Conference of 1885,
and the Brussels Conference of 1889 when the powers pledged themselves to
suppress slavery and the slave trade. They were on the whole unsuccessful.
It was not until 1926 when a Convention of the League of Nations made
slavery illegal that any serious effort was made to abolish the practice
world-wide.

No doubt it still exists in many isolated pockets in Africa and Asia.
In Oman on the Persian Gulf it was reported by a first-hand account in 1957,
when James Morris was a witness to the slaves held by the Sultan. "In 1956
the United Nations considered ways of preventing slave traffic in the
Indian Ocean, the Persian Gulf, and the Red Sea, through which numbers of
Negro slaves were reaching Saudi Arabia", evidence that it was in fact
still "prevalent over the entire Arabian Peninsula", for "the Saudis did
not see anything reprehensible in slavery".[8]

From this brief survey of the history of slavery, only one conclusion is possible. There was always a tendency on the part of large segments of the population to enslave others. "Man's inhumanity to man" is nowhere better exemplified than in the oldest, the longest, and the most persistent tradition of slavery.

Even after slavery in a formal sense was abolished in most of the world, other and more subtle forms took its place. The control by the masters of the Soviet Union of the masses of Russians, while not comparable with slavery in the strict sense, certainly does contain large elements that can be read that way, and can, as a matter of fact be compared with the serfdom of the Czarist regimes of old Russia. Most Soviet citizens today are unable to travel or change their jobs; what else is this but a form of involuntary servitude? Those who are even now forbidden the essential freedoms and human rights, as the Helsinki Conference defined them, are to that extent slaves.

Notes

1 Alasdair Whittle, Neolithic Europe: A Survey (Cambridge 1985, University Press).
2 Iliad, xxiv. 752, vi. 427; Odyssey, ix.40.
3 Laws, 6.776e et passim.
4 1241b20. The same comparison is made in the Ethica Nichomachea, 61a35-b5.
5 77a7-8
6 The Deipnosophists, vi, 262-267.
7 Borys Lewytzkj, Die Rote Inquisition (Frankfort 1967), p. 76
8 Sultan in Oman (New York 1957, Pantheon), p. 132. But see also pp. 33, 101, 107, et passim.

Chapter 8

THE MASSACRISTS

Massacre can be defined as the wholesale murder of human beings. As a
form of human behavior it has existed for a long time; nobody knows for how
long because of the absence of written records; but it is certainly as old
as writing. The word massacre itself comes either from the Latin, macellum,
a butcher's shop, or from Old Low German, matsken, to cut in pieces. Never
an approved custom, it was, however, always a practice. It has even
inspired painters, such as Eugene Delacroix's "The Massacre of Chios" and
Picasso's "Guernica". In most ancient histories written before the
twentieth century, massacres are seldom mentioned and never indexed, which
is some indication of how much they were taken for granted as ordinary
occurrences. They were certainly known to have happened but were not
considered noteworthy, and if they were reported it was in the most casual
terms.

In the earliest records of wars of conquest, such as by the Sumerians
in the third millenium BC and the Akkadians a millenium later, the defeat
of the enemy armies was usually followed by the massacre of the inhabitants
of the captured towns. This practice was almost standard, and was repeated
by the Assyrians and Chaldeans of the first millenium BC, by the Hittites
from 1350 BC, and by the Medes and Persians of the Achaemenid Empire from
550 BC. So it went also for the Heroic Ages in India. The Greeks and
later the Teutonic knights of northern Europe, all were accomplished

massacrists.

Wars are more often than not accompanied by the slaughter of the defeated enemy; their troops were either killed outright or carried off into slavery. Many such massacres are recorded in the folk epics that have been preserved. Indeed it seems to have been standard procedure for the Egyptians and the early Hebrews. Though there was no accepted name for it, we have come to call it massacre. Not only was it the fate of the defeated soldiers but also of the inhabitants of the towns who were often punished with "fire and the sword".

Probably, based on such fragmentary written records as have survived from the most ancient civilizations, the massacre of the defeated peoples was the usual practice. Kings often had inscribed on their monuments how they slew their thousands; so that far from grudgingly admitting this, it was the usual boast. If the question of moral wrong-doing was ever raised, there is no record of it. The idea that human life as such is precious and should be preserved may be a late nineteenth century idea. It has not been carried out in practice, as the many total wars of the twentieth century have attested.

The most famous of all massacres are those recited in the early books of the Bible. The first officially recorded massacre occurs in Exodus 32: 27-29, where it is set down that the Levites were ordered each to "kill his brother, his friend, his neighbor. The Levites obeyed, and about three thousand of the people died that day". There were other episodes such as that of the slaughter of the Midianites in Numbers, 31:7 of the Amorites in Numbers, 32; and, where Moses gave the order, in Deuteronomy to "defeat the seven nations and put them to death". When Rome defeated Carthage in the third of their wars, the city was razed, its male inhabitants all massacred, and the women and children sold into slavery (146 BC).

In the fifth century AD the nomads of central Asia suddenly erupted into the civilized world of the Indo-Europeans peoples and eventually made a dark ages in Eurasia with their conquests and massacres. They were first felt along the Great Wall of China, which had been built to contain them, and in Mongolia north of the Gobi Desert. The invasion of the Huns into the Roman Empire in the 5th and 6th centuries was their last expression.

Genghis Khan, (1162-1227) came out of the Mongol and Tartar steppes. He invaded northern China and captured Peking in 1215. He also destroyed the Muslim empire of Khwarizm, which had included a large part of what is now Soviet Central Asia and Iran, and he was singly responsible for more mass-acres than any other monarch in history. The destruction of Kiev was a typical achievement of his hordes. Men were slaughtered, old people tortured, young women raped, and children ridden down and killed, until there was nothing left but rubble and festering bodies; so that finally the Mongols themselves had to avoid the place. In the thirteenth century, the Mongols under his leadership destroyed all those people and possessions for which they could find no use. They laid waste to Bokhara, they spread destruction and ruin the length and breadth of Khorassan, strangling, beheading, and stabbing, with remorseless fury the inhabitants of Merv. The city of Bamiyan met the same fate.

Timurlane (1336-1405) was born near Samarkand with a Turkish rather than a Mongol inheritance. His conquests stretched from southern Russia to Mongolia and south into Persia and Mesopotamia. He treated many of the conquered peoples to the barbarous massacres which almost identify the practice with his name. A convert to Islam, he invaded India where he caused the massacre of millions both on the banks of the Indus and in

Delhi.

The ferocity of both Genghis Khan and Timurlane and their savage behavior are by no means exceptional. It seems to have been the accepted practice in Asia to slaughter the populations of cities which had been defended by enemy armies.

Generally speaking, people do not take formal cognizance of their actions when these have a character of which they disapprove. There was no term for the general and indiscriminate slaughter of human beings until Tacitus' history in the first century AD, but as we have noted, the practice had been in effect long before that.

Massacre is a peculiarly human activity. Other animals do not kill each other in wholesale lots, only individually and as needed for food. But humans do, and with such frequency that it must be counted a recognizable form of behavior.

There must be some morality involved in the fact that when massacres do occur, they are forgotten as quickly as possible. Few except kings and emperors are proud of such behavior and so no others are likely to admit that it exists. Many of the earliest massacres, like so much in history, have left no records. Since massacres can occur only when there are large numbers, obviously it cannot have had a long history, for the ranks of early man were thin.

Certainly massacres were common enough in western Europe in the struggle between the Conservative Roman Catholic Church and the new Protestant movement. The wars of religion of the 16th century were notable for the slaughters conducted by both sides. Wallenstein's atrocities were too much even for the Catholics and he was dismissed, but the destruction of Magdeburg in 1631 by the troops of the Catholic League under

General Tilly was just as ferocious: 20,000 of its inhabitants were killed. The Protestants behaved just as badly when the Swedes under Gustavus Adolphus (1594-1632) depopulated the country by unspeakable atrocities.

In general the results of the Thirty Year's War (1618-1648) was to reduce the population of Germany by half. The city of Augsburg for instance declined from 80,000 inhabitants to 16,000. The atrocities that accounted for this state of affairs was not the work of any one army but of all those of the various nations involved.

Paul Johnson in his history of the modern world[1] has recorded the number of massacres which have taken place within the last sixty years. Listed in alphabetic order, massacres have occurred in the following countries: Algeria, Cambodia, Cameroons, China, Egypt, France, Germany, India, Indonesia, Israel, Japan, Poland, Spain, Uganda. That is quite an impressive record and covers a large geographic part of the world, making the practice indeed seem quite common, as indeed it has been.

Massacres around the world are still almost everyday affairs, though such events are seldom acknowledged. The intent is to hide them or forget them, almost as though what we do not admit does not exist. An informal count yields a list of some sixteen such events in the first 83 years of our century, and this list is probably not complete.

In 1915 an Armenian minority of one million Armenians were massacred by the Turks of the Ottoman Empire.[2]

In 1930 millions of small Russian farmers, the Kulaks, were slaughtered on orders from Stalin.

In 1931-32 in the Ukraine 7 million were deliberately starved in a government-induced famine.

In 1931 the slaughter of Chinese, and in particular the citizens of

Nanking, was effected by the Japanese army, continuing until 1938.

The melancholy account of Stalin's murders of his competitors in the
Party and others, often with the secret connivance of Hitler, from 1936 to
1938 has been well documented. It accounted for more than $2\frac{1}{2}$ million people.
From 1936 to 1938, eight million Russians died in slave-labor camps.

In 1941, there was a massacre of Poles by the Russians in Katyn Forest.
War is always a fertile occasion for massacres, and the mass murder of helpless soldiers taken prisoner is quite common. Massacres were every-day
procedures in world war 2; the massacre of the French at Oradur, etc. Rules
of war, such as the Geneva Convention, were made only to be broken. The
ruthlessness of human intent when enemies are involved makes it quite easy
to destroy them in the most cold-blooded way.

The abstract nature of mass killing seems more like an efficiency
operation than like murder. The bombing of civilian cities was carried out
on both sides in world war 2 when none of the aviators could see the effect
of their missions, though thousands died as a result, including of course
women and children. This is a form of massacre, though it has seldom been
so described.

Certainly the largest as well as the best documented massacre of modern
times was the systematic and planned extermination of 6 million European
Jews by Hitler and the Nazis, from 1942 to 1945, known as the Holocaust.
It was heralded by the execution of 70,000 Germans who had been deemed
chronically insane or incurable. The "final solution" to be achieved by
the gassing in extermination camps planned for the purpose was finally
achieved with the destruction of some six million Jews in five death camps.
Such planned genocide on such a large scale was never attempted before, and
it is a commentary on the condition of human progress that it has happened

in our time.[3]

The massacre of the European Jews did not mean that the practice of massacre ended there, even though in 1949 the United Nations approved a Genocide Convention. Incidentally it has never been ratified by the U. S. Senate. The term, genocide, intended to mean the annhilation of an entire people or group, was coined by Raphael Lemkin in 1944 to describe the Holocaust.

In 1947 on the occasion of Indian Independence, millions of Moslems were slaughtered by Hindus and millions of Hindus by Moslems, many on trains operating between India and the new state of Pakistan.

In 1965 the revolt against President Sukarno in Indonesia by the Indonesian Communist Party was "one of the great systematic slaughters of the twentieth century, "the age of slaughter", and may have involved as many as a million victims, many of them put to the torture.[4]

From 1945 to 1965, 20 million "counter-revolutionaries" were massacred by the Chinese communists.

In the mid 1970s 9,000 citizens were murdered by the military regime in Argentina.

In 1971, when Bangladesh moved toward independence, acting on orders from the President of Pakistan the army was directed in a campaign of terror that was responsible for the lives of a million Bengalis.[5]

From 1975 to 1977, Pol Pot's communists slaughtered more than a million of their own Cambodian citizens.

In 1979 over 8,000 people were executed by the Iranian followers of the Ayatollah Khomeini as "enemies of Allah".

From 1975 to 1983, 65,000 people were slaughtered by the North Vietnamese.

In 1982, in Hama, forces loyal to the Syrian President, Hafez Assad massacred 10,000 men, women and children who were members of the Muslim Brotherhood.

In 1984, in the Lebanon, 285 U. S. Marines were massacred in their barracks by unnamed assassins, probably from the P.L.O.

Mark Siljander of Michigan in the U. S. House of Representatives has placed in the Congressional Record an account of the horrors in Afghanistan performed by the Russians.[6] It included the brutal burning of 40 men, women and children in a town square, the holding of children over fires to make the parents talk, the execution of women, putting toy bombs in food bins, putting pens and watches set to explode on the road to tempt children to take them. These are things, remember, that are happening in our time.

In 1985 the army of Sri Lanka slaughtered thousands of Tamils.

Recently (1985) the Sandanistas, the Marxist government of Nicaragua, are reported to have executed thousands suspected of opposition to the Communist regime.[7]

In western Europe the tradition of humanism dictated that massacres are wrong, indeed that all the killing of human beings is wrong; and though that assumption is seldom a deterrent, at least it exists; but in Asia there is no such tradition. The single exception is Buddhism, which has never penetrated Russia.

Wars are of course always fertile occasions for the occurrence of massacres. When an army unit is ordered to herd together and shoot a group of civilians or of military prisoners, the action does not seem out of the way and is executed with despatch as just another job of work in the ordinary life of the soldier. What has been done and what is continuing to be done does not seem at all unusual; quite to the contrary. Thus it happens that massacres occur and no mention is made of them.

The rank and file of the military take orders, they don't make decisions. They obey the commands of their officers, who in turn are controlled by those higher up. In a word, mindless actions in response to commands are the usual behavior of soldiers in the field.

What men in groups do is no different from what they do individually; massacres are simply murders writ large, and somehow, the factor of justification seems not to have been required. When a soldier is ordered to kill, provided many others have received the same orders at the same time, it almost seems to belong to the nature of things as a justified procedure.

Has anyone yet been interviewed on the topic? No soldier who took part in a mass killing would want to admit it afterwards and be consulted about his feelings at the time, but he would probably say that it had never occurred to him not to do what his officers had ordered. The death and the dying of others is a common element in the social environment. In every war, to be surrounded by corpses is the usual thing. To add to it, then, is an ordinary assignment.

There has not been to my knowledge any stated defense of the practice of massacre as such, though some political positions could be interpreted that way. If the members of an army battalion considered that they had been ordered to shoot down a bunch of prisoners who had until captured been intent on their destruction, it is not too difficult to conceive that they would feel they were acting in self-defense against a people who, if the tables had been turned, would have done the same thing to them. And they would have been quite right; the rules made governing warfare in the effort to render it "more humanitarian" were always foolish because they were undertaken to legislate actions that lay outside the law.

The slaughter of masses of human beings by other human beings, in short, may be considered a time-honored species of behavior. The records are of course incomplete, but they do show evidence that all societies contain in their histories at least some such occasions.

It would appear from the details of the foregoing account that massacre, the practice of genocide or of mass slaughter, is not only an ancient one but very much still on the increase; either that, or better records are being kept due to the progress of communication. In any case there has been no improvement.

Those who have not participated in a massacre must still share the guilt of those who have in virtue of a common humanity. It is not enough to disapprove of the practice even though the disapproval be expressed in the strongest terms. We have noted how often massacres have taken place in our own day and at the hands of our fellow man, and that makes it imperative not merely to voice our concern but to take steps to prevent further such behavior. It is up to us what those steps should be. At present, however, we do nothing at all, which is a form of acquiesence.

Notes

1 Modern Times (New York 1985), passim.
2 Congressional Record -- Senate for October 30, 1985, S14401 et seq.
3 A vast literature has grown up since the Holocaust, examining the phenomena from every perspective. A quick look at the details is available in Paul Johnson, Modern Times (New York 1983, Harper & Row), pp. 413-422. But also see Martin Gilbert, The Holocaust (New York 1986, Holt, Rinehart & Winston). Robert H. Abzug's Inside The Vicious Heart (New York 1986, Oxford University Press) offers a first-hand account of what the American soldiers saw when they liberated the concentration camps.
4 Paul Johnson, Modern Times, p. 480.
5 Nikolai Tolstoy, The Minister and the Massacres (London 1986, Hutchinson).
6 For September 18, 1985, E 4089-4091.
7 Associated Press dispatch of September 19, 1985.

Chapter 9

THE MURDERERS

For those of us who are fortunate enough to have lived in a comparatively peaceful time and place, such as the continental United States since
the end of the Civil War in 1865, most of the destructive effects of human
actions have occurred elsewhere. It is true that wars have cost American
lives in southeast Asia, but here at home there has been no such violence.
That is the case, certainly, with massacres and all collective human
aggression.

The same cannot be said, however, for individual murders. These occur
all around us on an almost daily basis. So common are they that we hardly
glance at the accounts in our daily newspapers and view them without comment
on our television news programs. This has a deep significance that has not
been explored. What does it mean to think of murder as an inevitable part
of society? Habit is a wonderful adjuster of values. What we experience
every day we can do little to change, or so we suppose; and so we accept it
as a usual condition of the social environment. This clearly will not do,
so perhaps it will help if we take a closer look.

If my thesis is correct, that a certain amount of violence is inherent
in human nature, then we can expect it to find some outlet even in a
comparatively peaceful society. The heritage of the hunting culture still
lives in all of us and is always just below the surface. The more tightly

animals are crowded together into a small living space, the more likely they
are to attack each other. Thus in our cities crime, and murder in particular, occurs with greater frequency than it does in more open communities.

In most cultures, if not in all, murder is a crime, and crimes are acts
committed in violation of a law which authorizes punishment for its
commission. Robbery is perhaps the commonest, with murder a close second.
There are no exact statistics to back up these statements because so many
offenses of both kinds go unreported, but there are enough to indicate its
prevalence.

According to the statutes, murder is the unlawful killing of another
human being with malice. The history of murder would probably coincide with
the history of man. As we have noted in chapter 2, there were deliberate
killings among early members of the human species, but of course there are no
records of motives. One of the first recorded murders is that of Abel by
Cain, in Gen. 4:9. Also the first lie is told about it in 4:10-11. Homicide,
the more usual term, is a frequent occurrence in countries with large
populations. Hardly a day passes in any big city without the police blotter
registering a number of such events. In a typical year in the United States,
say 1948, the Department of Justice reported 13,010 criminal homicides. Presumably there were many more not reported.

As we might expect, there are many reasons for murder. Professional
killers abound, but also many other kinds. Among the reasons, randomly listed,
are: revenge, hatred, gain, impulse, cult obligation, profit, fear, anger,
distrust, jealousy, delusions.

I assume that there are also many occasions for murder. Typical occasions
are: those committed in pursuit of a felony; to gain a political advantage,
or merely to exercise a power which can be expressed in no other way. In

many cases the murderer is known to his victim; very often he or she is a member of the same family. It is not after all so unusual a procedure. Murder as a common crime has been studied by experts[1] but I am concerned here to examine it as so typical an exaggeration of traits in human nature that it falls into the category of expected behavior.

Konrad Lorenz has called attention to the fact that animal aggression, "the fighting instinct in beast and man which is directed against members of the same species",[2] also plays a part in the preservation of the species.[3] Aggression is violent activity, usually performed by the male. The male is physically stronger than the female, and has muscles which periodically make their demands. These were used conventionally when primitive man hunted because it was his only way of obtaining food; but since he has moved into cities and left the extreme exercise of the muscles to a few professionals, with most of the heavy work done by machines, he feels a certain amount of frustration. Some of it is siphoned off by sport but not all and certainly not enough. The demand accumulates at a rate which has never been examined, until nothing less than a war will do. The original cause of murder may be attributed to the over-restrained musculature due to its unfitness to cope with the passivity required of the individual by a sedentary civilization which the individual is expected to endure without overt protest. The result is aggression, defined as the alteration of some part of the immediate environment by force. All human action therefore is a variety of aggression. It is ultimately irreducible in any animal that seeks to survive.

I have discussed aggression before in these pages and will so do again. It is the core conception in the understanding of human nature in its most active phase. The topic has been well explored in many recent studies[4] but no solution has yet been found, probably because it is needed for survival.

In any given population, a certain number will incline toward crimes of violence, including murder; probably those exhibiting evidence of an unbalanced nature. Isocrates, the Greek orator, wrote in 354 BC, (in the Antidosis, 274) that "the kind of art which can implant honesty and justice in depraved natures has never existed, and does not now exist".

Here I must mention again Freud's death instinct but take exception to it for the explanation of murder. Freud declared that every living organism is instinctively driven toward death,[5] which would make of aggression an inescapable impulse. According to this explanation there would be no accounting for life and for the instinct of every individual to survive.

Freud's chief error was his attempt to account for the normal in terms of the abnormal. Health cannot be explained away as an aberration of illness, and no sound osteology could be constructed on the basis of broken bones. Statistically, the suicides account for only a small part of the population. Most people want most anxiously and desperately to live, not to die. Murder can often be interpreted as an extreme step taken in the effort to survive by doing away with those suspected of a threat to survival.

Murder is not an expression of the death instinct but of a desperate attempt to express life; as the murderer sees it, the life of the murderer exchanged for the life of the victim exacted as the price that has to be paid. It often happens that due to circumstances, which may or may not have been under the individual's control, he feels out of things, "In instances of extreme alienation, which places the individual on some kind of social continuum where he is almost emotionally dead and totally disaffected, he uses violence to validate his existence".[6] In a word, he resorts to murder in the attempt to get himself back into the main stream.

Murder is the expression of extreme individual aggression. More often than not it is an impulsive action, the explosive reaction to a seemingly impossible situation.[7] It usually occurs without premeditation and has no further intended consequences. It is often followed by suicide because the aggression itself may be unfocused and so is easily turned against the self. In England in 1965, of every three murders one was followed by suicide.[8] Again in that typical year in the United States, 1948, 16,000 people committed suicide, 11.2 for every 100,000 population. Added to these numbers are the uncounted unsuccessful attempts which probably run into the tens of thousand.

Suicide is of course a form of murder —— the murder of the self. Durkheim ascribed it to one of three causes: altruistic, to benefit others; egoistic, to express failure to reach personal goals; and anomic, from the loss of social support in a disintegrating society.[9]

These are social motives for suicide; there is also the individual motive. Chief perhaps among these is the escape from pain. In an individual who suffers and who learns that he has an incurable disease from which he must eventually die and must in the meantime face almost certain increase in pain, there seems little other choice. Society has refused him help in this enter-prise, and he knows that he must accomplish it on his own. There is then no alternative to suicide, or so it seems to him.

Murder occurs when an individual suffers more aggression than his society can sustain and so he goes against it, making his protest by means of the destruction of whoever has occasioned his antagonism.[10] In a sense, though certainly not in a moral sense, he is as much its victim as the one whose life he takes.

Murder is the private version of what in a war takes public expression, a small-sized massacre, so to speak. When no social vehicle is available,

as in peace time, the individual driven by an ungovernable impulse, takes
matters into his own hands and commits a murder. That these are often family
affairs shows the intimate character of the crime. We have seen that there
are other kinds, but the close-in type reveals more surely the nature of
murder since there are no extraneous elements to dilute the motive.

In every society a certain number of individuals will suffer from para-
noid schizophrenia. Many of these will be murderers.[11] Defective organisms
rather than social conditions are likely to be causes. In recent studies of
excessively violent individuals, of the 321 examined, Dr. Frank Eliot of
Philadelphia reported that more than 90% showed evidence of brain dysfunction
and neurological defects.[12] Poverty is not responsible for murders, as
statistics show; indeed the crime rate rises with the rise in prosperity.[13]
The prevention of murder therefore cannot be found simply in the reformation
of society; it lies deeper in human nature.

All behavior patterns are to some extent culturally determined. Although
murder occurs in all cultures, in few is murder condoned or approved; but the
type and degree of punishment varies from culture to culture.

You might expect in fact discover that in no culture would murder be
accepted, in no culture would everyone turn aside from a murder and not
judge it a crime. But such is the wonderful variety of human nature that you
would be wrong. Probably every attitude that <u>can</u> be taken toward murder <u>has</u>
been taken at some time and place or other. Among the Ik, the mountain
people of Uganda, for instance, it is customary to leave the ill to die, and
in other similar ways commit what in effects amounts to murder.[14] The
customs and attitudes of the Ik lie at one end of the spectrum of human
behavior, which runs from absolute altruism to absolute selfishness, with the
Ik having what amounts to a monopoly of the selfish end.

In recent decades a new form of murder has been devised. Hijacking air-planes and killing some of the passengers, kidnapping individuals from streets and motor cars and later murdering them, all are comparatively new enterprises, new because the vehicles had not been invented earlier. Many of the murderers are religious fanatics, usually from some Moslem cult of extremists but not confined to them. Murder is murder, and in every case in the Lebanon the victims were helpless individuals. Iranians and more recently Libyans have taken the lead in this cowardly form of crime.

No one has ever supposed that murder can be eliminated altogether. Robbery, is probably here to stay, and all we can hope to do is to reduce its frequency by increasing the penalty. But murder is too common a procedure, too impulsive an action, too widespread a remedy of supposed wrongs, ever to disappear as a human alternative. The most that can be hoped for is that the number of such incidents can be reduced. We have one index: where punishment is lax, the number of murders increase; where it is severe, they tend to lessen.[15] The conclusion is obvious: increase the penalty for murder gradually until the point is reached where the severity is no greater a deterrent; then hold it there.

Notes

1 Richard J. Herrnstein and James Q. Wilson, Crime and Human Nature (New York 1985, Simon & Schuster).
2 On Aggression (New York 1966, Harcourt, Brace & World), p. ix.
3 Ibid., chapter 3.
4 E.g. Gerda Siann, Accounting for Aggression (London 1985, Allen & Unwin).
5 Beyond the Pleasure Principle (London 1948, Hogarth Press), p. 47
6 Louis S. B. Leakey, "Development of Aggression As A Factor in Early and Pre-Human Evolution", in C. D. Clemente and D. B. Lindsley (eds.) Aggression and Defence (Berkeley 1967, University of California Press), p. 25
7 M. B. Clinard, Sociology of Deviant Behavior (New York 1957, Holt, Rinehart & Winston), p. 210.
8 D. J. West, Murder Followed by Suicide (London 1965, Heinemann), p. 150.

102

E. Durkheim, <u>Suicide</u>, J. A. Spaulding and G. Simpson, trans. (New York 1951, Free Press).

K. Lorenz, <u>On Aggression</u>, ch. 11.

11 Anthony Storr, <u>Human Aggression</u> (London 1968, Allen Lane, The Penguin Press), p. 96, and ch. 11.

12 These and similar statistics from a symposium on the topic were reported in the <u>New York Times</u> for September 17, 1985.

13 <u>Crime and Human Nature</u>, p. 327 f.

14 Colin M. Turnbull, <u>The Mountain People</u> (New York 1972, Simon & Schuster), pp. 151-154, but cf. <u>passim</u>.

15 <u>Crime and Human Nature</u>, p. 343.

Chapter 10

THE TORTURERS

1. Introduction

Torture is the act of inflicting excruciating pain, intended as punishment for a supposed wrong, as an act of revenge, as a method of extracting a
confession, or for the enjoyment of cruelty. It is the ultimate tort or
injury to the person, a means of "getting even" or a weapon to inspire fear
and induce conformity. A special sexual version called Sadism, after the
Marquis de Sade in the eighteenth century, and known medically as algolagnia,
has received attention as a sexual perversion.

Torture is, in short, the greatest extreme to which aggression can go
short of murder. "Aggression and human violence have marked the progress of
our civilization and appear, indeed, to have grown so during its course that
they have become a central problem of the present",[1] probably a consequence
of the fact, noted in chapter 2, that "the age of the hunter, the
Paleolithic, comprises by far the largest part of human history".[2]

Torture is prevalent in periods of cultural change. Despite this,
however, most texts devoted to a study of the range of human behavior do not
include it. Due to its nature it rarely comes to the attention of the
general public. For obvious reasons, those who engage in it do not want the

facts known, and therefore accurate information is difficult to obtain.

Still, the evidence we do have is overwhelming. This is attested by the careful work of Amnesty International in their recent publication, Torture in The Eighties,[3] and by other sources, such as that of Craig Pyes in the Albuquerque Journal between December 18 and 22, 1983. Amnesty International has collected the evidence that 100 governments, roughly one fourth of all the governments in the world today, routinely practice torture.

The deliberate use of torture is certainly a recurrent human activity. Anthropologists report it as quite common among primitive cultures.[4] If the evidence furnished by primitive societies and advanced civilizations is to be accepted, then such cruelty is a constant, for there is no less in the one than in the other. The history of torture is a long and melancholy affair.[5] There are accounts of it in many previous civilizations. Torture was an accepted practice in ancient Greece and Rome, where it was usually employed on slaves and metics either by way of punishment for an infraction or to extract a confession. Both Aristotle and Demosthenes thought it a reliable means of obtaining evidence, and it was at least recognized as an established practice by Aristophanes and Isocrates.

The Roman system recognized torture as a regular procedure and so it became the basis of later practice. The Catholic Church though at first opposed to torture finally accepted it and even relied on it. From the fourth century in Europe onwards torture was variously employed, though it did not come to full power until the fifteenth century with the Spanish Inquisition under the leadership of Torquemada and supported by the Dominican order. It is a well known fact that at least two thousand persons were burned at the stake during Torquemada's lifetime. Strangling was also employed, and there were many instruments designed for various kinds of torture, such as the Rack, the Boot and the Iron Maiden.[6]

In Asian countries torture has always been quite common, having been usually employed at the whim of an absolute monarch. In more recent times it was practiced in Europe. Gibbon recounts the blinding by Basil the Second, in 1014, the conqueror of the Bulgarians, of 15,000 captives.[7] The Greeks of Adramtthium in the time of Malek Shah (1106-16) Turkish children in boiling water.[8] There is a description of the terrible cruelties accompanying the massacres of Armenians by the Turks in the 19th century, revealing, in Dillon's words, "the unimagined strata of malignity in the human heart."[9]

Torture in the modern world has become almost a commonplace. It was practiced in Indonesia by the Communist Party thre (the PKI). In Algeria in the 1950s, torture was systematically employed on both sides.[10] But perhaps the Russians get the grand prize because they have had a larger and more powerful country and have been at it longer. The Soviet Union is known to have used their camps for torture as well as extermination.[11] Medvedev puts the total figure of those tortured and killed as 10 million.

The refinement of torture has continued into our day, utilizing many of the inventions which were not formerly available. Thus electric prods devised for the control of cattle are now used on prisoners. When Hitler caught his enemies he hung them on meat hooks. The KGB is not known for the gentle treatment of those it interrogates. The torture of political prisoners is currently a routine procedure in Russian prison camps, as reported from many sources.[12] The Russians, who have superimposed a Marxist doctrine on a Czarist society, are known to continue the procedure, but they are not alone. The practice is prevalent, as the evidence collected by Amensty International shows.[13] The Russians are reported currently (October 1984) to have thrown nude Afghan women out of airplanes as retaliation for the bombing of military installations.

Others as well as communists rely upon torture as a regular practice. It was evidently a specialty of the Argentine generals who were in power before the Falklands War. In other countries the secret police engage in it.

The point is that torture is so well established as a human activity and so prevalent, that it must have a basis in some human need, and I plan to investigate it from this point of view.

2. The Organic Theory of Motivation

Perhaps the best place to start the inquiry is by looking into the nature of human action in general. That may give us a clue to the understanding of its extremes.

All other human activities are broadly speaking forms of aggression, if we define aggression as the effort to alter by force something in the material environment. This may take one of two forms: constructive, when something is built, or destructive, when something is destroyed. Such a scheme suffers from being too simple, of course; cutting down trees to build a house involves both; but they do come in purer varieties, as for example in the work of the artist or the soldier.

The life of an organism consists in various drives aimed at reducing its needs, reflexive responses to materials in the immediate environment. Thus every overt activity can be interpreted as a reaction to an object,[14] one requiring material things from the environment for which deliberate efforts of aggression have to be made.

Among the familiar needs are those for water, food and sex. Each is a requirement of some special organ of the body: water for the kidneys, food for the stomach, sex for the gonads. Obtaining them calls on special drives and results in standard interchanges with the environment.

Information, security, and activity are less familiar. To obtain these there exists also special organs and drives: the brain for information, the skin for security, the muscles for activity.

Consider how all six needs operate through feeling: the lack of water is felt as thirst, the lack of food as hunger, the lack of sex as libido, the lack of information as curiosity, the lack of security as fear, the lack of activity as stiffness. The first three are concerned with immediate survival, the effort of the individual to stay alive, while the last three are occupied with ultimate survival and the effort to achieve immortality.

The six needs I have mentioned are not as separate as my list would indicate. It requires a certain amount of curiosity to discover where water and food are to come from and to plan how they can be obtained, and it takes a certain amount of activity to procure them. The one that will occupy us the most here is the need of the muscles for activity. There is little indication of its presence, yet it is there in force and very vigorous when called on.

The special need of the muscles takes the form of aggression, and may be defined as the effort to alter by force some material object in the environment. The need to do, to be active, exerts dominance, and under conditions of deprivation supports all the other drives. It is insistent and it is brutal, and in a certain sense automatic and unavoidable. In order to see the importance of the muscles in reducing the other needs, we have only to consider a typical one. Let us consider how hunger, the need of the stomach, is served.

The human species is carnivorous, which means the routine slaughter of animals for food. For most of mankind this procedure is carried out now by surrogates. The fisherman and the butcher are professionals who do our killing for us.

Men do not ordinarily engage in any practice for which there is no need. Torture can be seen as a quick fix for those who feel frustrated by the sedentary life as lived in the cities. It is not confined to the torturing of humans but includes other animals. How else describe game fishing? Tarpon rodeos are quite common and have no other purpose, since the flesh of the tarpon is inedible. Hunting is not limited to killing for food, either, but extends to wild animals not intended to be eaten, as happens for instance on safaris conducted for the shooting of lions and tigers.

What is the nature of such a need? I believe it can be found in the left-over drives aimed at need-reductions. We must look at these next if we are to understand the prevalence of torture.

3. The Left-Over Drives

One feature of the drives to reduce the organic needs is peculiar to man: they do not end when the needs are reduced. Instead he anticipates his needs and prepares to cope with them. Thus after a heavy meal knowing he will be hungry again he might purchase food for the coming days.

The results of such anticipation are the left-over drives. Their effects may be seen in water conduits and purification systems, in libraries, in farms and ranches, in slaughter houses, marriages and harems, in armies, and indeed in all of the institutions and arrangements requisite for anticipating the reduction of future needs.

It is worth understanding, then, that in every one of his efforts at need-reduction, man endeavors to exceed himself. Remember, then, that with him, unlike the other animals, a drive does not stop when a need is met.

Consider the sexual need for example. The Don Juan phase of collecting conquests has been extended in former times to multiple marriages and even to harems. Any drive may of course occupy an individual's entire supply of energy, and so become the principle reason for his existence. This blocking effect produces the exaggerated actions which the ancient Greeks recognized so clearly as "outrageous behavior", but it produces also all the selfless devotion to altruistic causes and the monuments of art, religion and science.

In any typical sample of a large population, most activities will belong to the average of ordinary aggression, but the extremes will not. At one extreme lie the pacifists and vegetarians; at the other the torturers.

Such limited practices are not in themselves indicative of the size of the problem, for the responses made to a need often exceed the stimulus provided by the material objects which provoked it. In the long run nothing less than the conquest and domination of the entire environment will suffice. Thus we see as products of the left-over drives the whole of material civilizations. Unfortunately, we can see also in the unbounded ambitions of the individuals composing it the drives which make it unstable.

It sometimes happens that the drives to reduce the needs do not reach their objects. Those that do not end by producing emotions. Much of the emotional life is connected with the inhibition of some strong need, some organic drive which has not been carried out in action. Emotion generally speaking is the response of the whole organism to the blocking of behavior.

Any organ deprivation may be the occasion for the expression of an emotion. Perhaps the most common is fear, which arises from a threat to continued existence. Rage is the outcome of actions of a violent nature which had been expected by the muscles but not performed; similarly, anger is the result of withheld action. Torture follows when hate and hostility result from fixing on a particular object as the cause of a frustration, though this is not the only or even the principal reason.

4.   Torture As A Left-Over Drive

We can easily, see, then, how the practice of torture fits into the theory of organic motivation and the left-over drives. If too long inactive the muscles express themselves with over-compensating vigor, bursting out in violence. Hence the effects of the left-over drives can be destructive as well as constructive. Destructive aggression of this sort would not be satisfied by the death of a victim; there must be revenge. The need for aggression can take many forms, such as happens in wars. It is well known that prisoners who were killed were often tortured first. Torture in war and even in peace is quite common.

Torture may be classified, then, as the ultimate expression of destructive aggression, the response that deliberately administers pain. Several kinds may be distinguished. One follows anger and occurs in the heat of passion, but the other is the result of calculated hostility and is a cold and continuing response. The inflicting of pain or injury to another organism reduces a need in the aggressor. Only a program of torture offers the promise of such need-reduction in the future.

As one product of the ultimate state of arousal, the pleasure at the

pain of another must be counted high on the list. The torturer probably
recognizes as he listens to the outcries of his victims the element of
negative empathy involved, as though saying silently to himself, "This is
happening to him and not to me", and he enjoys it. What satisfies a need
will not be so easy to dispose of, and so we must seek to gain a greater
understanding of the problem.

5. Nature of The Difficulty

The more cultivated people are, the more they believe that torture
should not occur. What then should be done to prevent it?

It is probably useless to look to the average individual, the "man of
good will" to eliminate the use of torture in the name of conscience.
"Conscience" is merely the standing readiness to engage in the self-
criticism which follows any infraction of an accepted morality, and could as
easily lead to the approval of torture as to protests against it. If for
instance a terrorist was arrested who was known to have planted a bomb that
was timed to go off the next day and kill a number of innocent people,
almost anyone would approve of his torture to extract a confession.

Perhaps the greatest obstacle to the improvement of the human condition
is man's persistent refusal to recognize that he himself is the problem.
Man as an animal is comparatively new to the sedentary life, which, organi-
cally, does not quite suit him. His muscles were designed not to be
circumvented but to be used to their utmost. Hence the periodic outbursts
of violent action, such as happens sometimes with individuals and always in
war.

In the long period of history from early to modern man, there has been

immense progress in technology but none at all in motivation. He has
learned to reduce his needs more efficiently, but the needs have remained
much the same.[15] The two conflicting motives of the individual have been
to help and hurt his fellows. Each has had its artifacts to match: From
the medicine man of the primitive tribe with his herbs and incantations,
whose aim was to heal, and the warrior with his bows and arrows, whose aim
was to kill, to the modern counterparts of the doctors with their hospitals
and the soldiers with their nuclear weapons, it is easy to see that while
the means have been improved, the ends have not changed.

Thus man has had built into the very structure of his life cycle the
constancy of his opposite aims, and he pursues the one as avidly as the
other. That the conflict between them is self-defeating is not lessened
by the fact there is a rhythm to history which allows them to alternate.
For constructive and destructive aggression have each had its historical
justification. We think of modern medicine as human while we think of war
as inhuman, but the fact is that the one is as human as the other. If wars
can be justified, then so can torture.

What is the answer? I have no ready one to suggest. Other animals
hold down a population which otherwise might get out of hand by means of
the food chain; each species is eaten by a higher; but there is no species
higher than man, at least not on our planet, and the task therefore is
turned over to wars, which function as the oldest human method of population control.

Here I must make a contrast between this method practiced by man and
the one practiced by other animals. For other animals the food chain is
a useful device: not only are the herds kept down to reasonable numbers
but the breed is improved. Note for example that when lions feed on

antelope it is the weakest that are caught and eaten. But man's method of holding down the population is to engage in war, where the opposite is true, for in war only the best and strongest are drafted and sent into battle. Wars do reduce the population but only by depressing the breed.

It is every individual's view that there must be a better way, but thus far none has been suggested. Moreover, the technology of war has been developed to the point that where if continued it could easily lead to the total destruction of the species.

It has not been sufficiently recognized that in every society there is a cross-section of human individuals with skewed needs. Together their activities represent the total life of the culture, but they differ markedly among themselves. Some are benevolent, while others are violent and aggressive. Now societies must find places for such extreme cases. Some who are benevolent enter the practice of medicine, work in nursing homes, or engage in charities of some institutional variety. Others more destructively inclined choose the army.

Such extreme elements exist in every society. Those who labor to reduce the amount of pain in the world speak for themselves. But so long as nations continue to rely on wars to settle their differences the retention of the military will be essential and the role of aggressive individuals assured. Since the need for destructive violence is organ-specific, only the overcoming of physical resistance by force will reduce the insistent need of the muscles and bring peace to the organism.

In a word, torture as a need-reducing procedure will remain, and it seems likely to continue as a feature of social life until a substitute can be found for it, however much those with altruistic feelings object. We may be filled with horror at the spectacle of homo hominis lupus, yet no useful purpose is served by hiding the facts. We must face the needs of the musculature and recognize them for what they are. Only then can the problem of torture be dealt with directly, for it is a recurrent one.

6. A Profile of The Torturer

Perhaps we should ask ourselves, what is the torturer really like? It will be useful to begin by comparing torture with terrorism, particularly since both have become features of our critical times. Terrorism involves the inflicting of pain on those ordinarily beyond reach and is usually a one-time event involving a number of victims. Torture, on the other hand, is a sustained series of episodes in which pain is inflicted separately on captives who are susceptible indefinitely or until death intervenes.

The torturer has rarely felt a need for justification but he is usually able to persuade himself that if he did not do this to the victim, under other circumstances it would have been done to him. Torture or be tortured is his conviction, and under it he practices his cruelty as a skill, using instruments that were designed for the purpose that clearly demonstrate it to be a well-established practice.

Both terrorism and torture are the work of absolutists. Now as we have seen already in chapter 6 the absolutist is a fanatic believer who, powered by an uncritical zeal wishes to impose his beliefs upon others, or, failing that, to kill them because he is convinced that his faith justifies his actions. The fanaticism of the absolutist inevitably leads to terrorism and torture, terrorism as inflicted on those ordinarily beyond reach, and torture as inflicted on those within his control.

Absolutists are to be found chiefly in religion and politics.

Fundamentalism in religion, of whatever denomination, tends to take on this character, the belief in a divine person or a creed as an assured fact and thus the ground for certainty. It is based on an absolute belief which is usually assumed to be exclusive and rare, whereas it is actually the cheapest thing in the world. Absolute belief exists in many of the world religions but also in politics, in monarchies for instance, and, more lately, in many varieties of Marxism, though nationalism is not free from it.

We need to distinguish the professional killer from the other absolutists. It is when the killer turns against his own kind that the trouble starts, and he seems able to do this when he is provoked by differences in belief. Killing out of conviction is after all only carrying such beliefs to their logical end. We must learn how to persuade the killer of his own kind not to kill for his beliefs, that is the essence of the problem. And we can do so evidently only by persuading him that his beliefs are not supported by certainty and are therefore not absolute.

The evidence for this contention is to be found in the distinction between the two ontological domains, the one of logic and the other of matter. In the domain of logic and mathematics the absolute truth of tautologies is quite common; in the domain of matter it does not exist: there are no absolutes in the material world. Therefore the "absolute truths" of religion and politics are misleading. This means that the terrorist and the torturer, whose actions have results which are final, are mistaking relative claims for absolute truths.

We must have beliefs strong enough to justify our actions, that is so; yet these should never constitute absolutes. If behavior is such that it always contains an element of doubt, then acts of terrorism and torture, and even more strongly, acts of war, would never be justified. We must learn therefore how to order our lives on the basis of probabilities. This will require a wholly new technique and a program to go with it, admittedly a very large ambition; yet nothing less will do.

Programs based on statistical trends would be sufficient to justify moderate actions yet eliminate the extremes by which torture is currently justified. It would enable people holding rival beliefs to live together in peace, and that alone would be worth any striving. Such a goal cannot be achieved overnight but in the meanwhile might be worth putting into practice as an ideal, for surely we cannot go on much longer as things are now with the amount of torture in the world serving as a measure of the extent to which we have fallen short of our highest capabilities.

Notes

1 Torture was formally condemned by draft treaty and passed by acclamation at the United Nations on December 6, 1984. See the New York Times of that date.

2 Walter Burkert, Homo Necans, translated by Peter Bing (University of California Press, Berkeley 1983), pp. 1,17.

3 London 1984, Amnesty International Publications.

4 E. g., S. L. Washburn, "Speculations of the Inter-relations of the History of Tools and Biological Evolution", in The Evolution of Man's Capacity for Culture, J. N. Spuhler, ed. (Detroit 1959, Wayne State University Press).

5 See e. g. Daniel P. Mannix, The History of Torture (New York 1983; Dell and Edward Peters, Torture (Oxford 1985, Blackwell). Henry Charles Lee, Torture (Philadelphia 1973, University of Pennsylvania Press), contains copies of the original legal documents authorizing torture.

6 Ency. Brit., 14th ed., vol. 22, pp. 311-314.

7 Edward Gibbon, The Decline and Fall of the Roman Empire (London 1898, Metheun(, vi, pp. 136-7.

8 T. A. Walker, History of The Law of Nations (1899), p. 124.

9 E. J. Dillon, (1868, Contemporary Review).

10 Jacques Soustelle, Aimee et souffrante Algerie (Paris 1956); Jacques Massu, La vrai bataille d'Alger (Paris 1971).

11 Simon Wolin and Robert M. Slusser, The Soviet Secret Police (New York 1957), p. 194; Antoni Ekart, Vanished Without a Trace (London 1954, p. 244; Roy Medvedev, Let History Judge: The Origins and Consequences of Stalinism (New York 1971), pp. 90-91 et passim.

12 The Wall Street Journal for December 21, 1984.

13 See their Report on Torture (London 1973, Duckworth). See also Eric Stover and Elena O. Nightingale, The Breaking of Bodies and Minds: Torture, Psychiatric Abuse and the Health Professions (San Francisco,

Calif., W. H. Freeman).

14 Cf. Sir Charles Sherrington, The Integrative Action of the Nervous System, second edition, (New Haven 1947, Yale University Press), p. x.

15 James K. Feibleman, "The Ambivalence of Aggression and The Moralization of Man", in Perspectives in Biology and Medicine. Vol. IX, No. 4.

Chapter 11

THE TERRORISTS

Terrorism is certainly a characteristic of our epoch, though I doubt that there have been many periods without some of it. In other chapters of this book I have noted that killing is common enough to mankind, but terrorism refers to a special kind of random killing which is usually unexpected. The practice is old enough if we mean only the surprise murder by members of the underground of selected victims as a protest against the social order.

Not all terrorists belong irrevocably to the underground. Felix Dzerzhinsky did; he spent 14 years in prison when the Okhrana, the Czarist secret police, captured him. When after the Revolution Lenin in 1918 asked him to organize the intelligence and security arm of the Bolshevik Party, he employed both former prisoners and former members of the Okhrana in a secret-police organization which preserved the party after Lenin's death as well as preparing for the Stalinist terror. Lenin, like Begin in Israel, began as a terrorist and ended as the open and acknowledged leader of his country. Stalin, whose victims have been estimated at some 10 million, was, you might, say a terrorist in power. Dzerzhinsky's heritage is the KGB, with its widespread network of spies and its terrorists training camps.[1]

Revolutions are organized attempts to overthrow governments. They are common enough in recent times, as witness the French Revolution in 1789, the American Revolution against the British in 1812, and the Russian Revolution of 1919. Such large changes are seldom peacefully arranged. This is not, however, what is meant now by terrorism, which is more often the work of small groups or even of individuals who disagree with the prevailing order and wish only to make inroads against it.

What is new now is the effort of some states to back terrorism as a way of disestablishing others, especially the work of the Soviet Union in training and equipping terrorists with the help of its satellite nations, Libya and Cuba.

Terrorists work in the dark or under some kind of concealment. When they are visible they wear masks. They prefer to kill by taking advantage of surprise and speed. They are single-minded and self-appointed killers who give their chosen enemy no warning. There is no hint in their actions of what they are defending and they often wish to have no identity if it can be avoided.

There is always plenty of money available to pay for the work of terrorists, much of it provided by Colonel Quaddafi of Libya, some from the Soviet Union, while other funds are furnished by dissident Arab states. The "Weather Underground" in the United States robbed banks to pay for its operations. Sometimes specific acts were rewarded and bonuses paid for them; generally, anyone who wished to move against Israel or the United States could find the necessary money. Destruction in any form does not come cheap.

Terrorists are always negative actors in the social drama. They create nothing, only destroy; they fill no vacuum. They are incapable of establish-ing social order, and it never seems to occur to them that existing govern-ments serve everyone and that most people are content with what they have and prefer it to what the terrorists are offering in exchange.

It is characteristic of terrorists that they seek only destruction.

Usually they confine their efforts to killing those they think are standing in the way of promoting some cause they do not accept, but often they seek a justification by taking hostages who are to be freed when some aim is accomplished, such as releasing political prisoners or providing funds. But the shadow of killing always comes through their efforts and colors them. Terrorists are people without conscience who are convinced of the rightness of their cause sufficiently to justify the violence of their actions. Their aims can be purely negative, as when as nihilists they call for the destruction of the hated institution of capitalism. They are by nature absolute believers, and so make common cause with others who do; Islam joining hands with Marxism.

All terrorists have some characteristics in common to matter what culture they come from. They are aggressive but also cowardly; they are entirely without conscience, since they frequently number among their victims women and innocent children; and they are usually ignorant, knowing little about the causes they profess to be serving. Those who are so completely committed to violent action have little inclination to devote time to thought or feeling, hence the single-minded nature of their cause.

In every population there is always a certain number of extreme personalities who are criminals and psychopaths.[2] They are usually dealt with by the police, the courts and the mental hospitals and jails. This is certaily true of well-established and orderly societies; but in times of trouble when the legitimacy of the ruling order in the state is under attack, the psychopath may come to the fore as a public-spirited hero whose work furthers the revolution advocated by others. Carefully segregated but supported in the Soviet Union, and almost publicly acknowledge in Iran, Libya and elsewhere among the satellites of communism, the psychopath becomes a terrorist and is given surreptitious support. His position may be described paradoxically as a partly-illegitimate legitimacy: legitimate to his sponsors, illegitimate to the social order he endeavors to undermine.

The more democratic the country, and the greater the number of freedoms available to its citizens, the more vulnerable it is to acts of terrorism. As Thomas P. Raynor points out, there is no terrorism practiced in fascist or communist countries where repressive regimes do not allow for any latitude of individual initiative.[3] He has shown that terrorism today may be racial, i.e. white against black; religious, as with the Ku Klux Klan against Roman Catholics and Jews; or national, as against legitimate governments.

Moreover, terrorism as a profession tends to spread, so that terrorists who began in one country could operate in others far away, so that now we have members of the PLO in Latin America, Chileans in the United States, Japanese in the Lebanon, Libyans in Egypt. The various terrorist groups join forces in a loosely organized federation which extends completely around the world. Terrorism has never succeeded in organizing itself into a well-knit and permanent group, but there is always that danger. There is enough ill will and there are enough governments to support it. Perhaps the very nature of the enterprise, which must count on concealment, limits its effectiveness.

However, the extent of the international cooperation among terrorists may have been underestimated. When in Philadelphia on May 25, 1985, the FBI agents arrested Dr. Alan Berkman of New York City and Ann Duke of Austin, Texas, they picked up two members of the May 19th Communist Movement, evidently an offshoot of the Weather Underground and linked to the Black Liberation Front, "all parts of the Marxist-Leninist revolutionary apparatus".[4]

In August of that same year it was recognized by the authorities in

Europe that the strategy of the terrorists had shifted to attacks on
military bases, particularly those of the Americans but not exclusively.
There was no longer any effort to avoid killing ordinary people in the
bombings of those they considered their class enemies. These included army
privates as well as the manufacturers of weapons of war, both the work of
groups called the French Direction Action and in West Germany the Red Army
Faction.[5]

Man was born to reason but he does put that faculty to strange uses.
Such is his nature that he feels called upon to defend by claim and argument
whatever program he undertakes. The most quoted statement on the topic is
that of the Russian, Bakunin. In his version of anarchism all government is
evil and must be destroyed. "The urge to destroy is a creative urge." He
never explained why but that has been the slogan of destroyers ever since.

No doubt he was a strong influence on Karl Marx, who thereby entered the
tradition of terrorism. Bakunin's most astute pupil was Nachaev who wrote
a Catechism of the Revolutionary. Like Bakunin, he advocated violence for
its own sake. It was Nachaev's idea that terrorists should organize themselves into very small groups so that no captured member would be in a
position to betray too many of his comrades under torture.

Acts of terrorism against heads of state were common in the last century.
Among the victims of assassination were: the Empress Elizabeth of Austria-
Hungary, President Carnot of France, King Umberto of Italy, President
McKinley of the United States, King Carlos I of Portugal. But in no single
case did the action bring down the government or have any lasting effect.
The only exception, the assassination of the Austrian Archduke, Franz
Ferdinand at Sarajevo in 1914, which precipitated world war 1, did not
produce independence for Serbia.

Wherever there are cultural differences, assassinations are invited, especially in times of social change. In our own day (1985) the assassinations continue: Armenian against Turk, Sikh against Hindu, Moslem against Christian, one Moslem faction against another, black against white, Roman Catholic against Protestant. There is always a specific charge, but the violence is always the same attempt to right an alleged wrong by commiting another wrong.

There have been no lack of terrorists in our century. Most notable and persistent have been the Irish seeking an end to British rule, beginning with the Fenian Brotherhood and continuing to this day with the IRA, the Irish Republican Army.

In Palestine, the Irgun Zvai Leumi, the National Military Organization, in which Menachem Begin participated, later intensified by the Stern gang, fought with the British to gain the Jewish independence of Palestine. The movement was destroyed by the British in a pitched battle, but its aims prevailed eventually in the establishment of a Jewish state.

The advent of the communist states accelerated the movements of terrorism around the world. This has been true of both the Soviet Union and communist China led by Chairman Mao, whose "little red book" advocated violence as the only way to gain revolutionary ends. Terrorism was given a justification by the "class struggle" in which every Marxist believes.

Terrorism spread and gained a new form, the urban guerilla, the work of a Spaniard named Abraham Guillen, whose Strategy of the Urban Guerilla, not published until 1966, had gained many advocates before that, thought the most influential was a Brazilian, Carlos Marighella, whose published version entitled Minimanual of the Urban Guerilla was even more popular with terrorists. For all of them, the only accomplishment necessary was negative:

to destroy: In this sense they are entitled to be considered the pure inheritors of Russian anarchism.

Elsewhere[6] I have traced the more recent advocacy of terrorism to a Russian who lived in France and passed on his influence to the French philosophers, Jean-Paul Sartre and Merleau-Ponty. Latin America too has had its share of terrorists. The Tupamaros of Uruguay succeeded in destroying the only genuine democracy that had appeared there. In Argentina the Montoneros were opposed by Peron, who saw in them an example of what he called "pathological barbarism".

In the United States the terrorist groups included, besides the Weather Underground in New York led by students from affluent homes, the Black Panthers in Chicago, and others.

In West Germany the Red Army Faction, more popularly called the Baader-Meinhof gang, operating independently were eventually destroyed by the police, but have had their successors, who are making themselves felt in attacks on American army installations.

In Italy the Red Brigades have operated and continue to operate, despite the arrest of 140 members.

In the Lebanon for some time the situation has been confused and out of control. There are many sides: Moslem against both Moslem and Christian; Christian against Moslem; Israeli against Moslem; to say nothing of independent guerillas. Bombing seems to be the preferred expression, from the destruction of the Israeli athletes in the 1972 Olympics by the "Black September" terrorists and the attack on 241 American Marines in the Lebanon in October 1983, to the highjacking of the TWA passengers airplane Flight 847 there this year (1985).

An interesting spectacle of our time is the making of common cause by fanatical Moslems and atheistic communists, in the efforts of the leaders of the Soviet Union, the Russians supplying training camps and weapons. There is good orthodox Marxist justification for this activity. After all, Marx himself had approved of terrorism as means of furthering the revolution. "Violence itself is an economic power", he wrote.[7]

As was inevitable, the various terrorist groups found that they had a common aim: to destablize the Western democracies they regarded as capitalist foes. After all, they had a common sponsor. The result was that at the Tricontinental Congress organized in Havana, Cuba in 1966, some five hundred delegates took part. I quote the list of delegates from Raynor's account: the Black Panthers, the Quebec Liberation Front, the IRA, the Baader-Meinhof group, Japan's United Red Army, Croatian Separatists from Yugoslavia, the Peoples' Liberation Army from Turkey, the PLO and the Spanish Basque terrorists.[8]

Their efforts were to be paid for by the vast sums accumulated through bank robberies and extortion practices as well as from funds furnished by the Arab oil countries. Cuba remained a center of training camps under the direction of the KGB, but there were others located in Algeria, Iraq, Jordan, the Lebanon and South Yemen. Most of the weapons of course came from the Soviet Union and Czechslovakia.

Raynor is careful to point out that the Russians distinguish between terrorists acting on behalf of "national liberation" movements and those acting on their own, intending to support only the former; though the distinction has been a difficult one to maintain.[9]

The future of terrorism is grim for those nations it aims to overthrow. There is always the possibility that terrorist groups will construct or be given chemical or biological weapons or even nuclear bombs, all difficult to

monitor or control. Could such a group actually build a nuclear bomb? This
would not be easy, for it would require considerable skill; still, the
possibility remains. How could such a threat be anticipated and the danger
diffused? No one yet knows the answer, though authorities in all Western
countries are very much concerned.[10]

Certainly all agree that the vast attention given to terrorists by the
mass media: the newspapers, radio and television, serves no good purpose.
The recognition of the terrorists and their violent and aggressive acts
seems to lend a kind of legitimacy that is sure to encourage their efforts.
Perhaps this is not what the media intended but it is what they accomplish.
No country with a free press wants to establish curbs. The only hope is that
the media will engage in self-censorship and so accomplish the same aim but
without repression.[11]

It is highly significant that there is no terrorism in the Soviet Union,
as indeed there had been none in Mussolini's Italy or in Nazi Germany.
Repressive regimes in which the government itself constitutes a standing
terror have nothing to fear from rival terrorists, for everyone in a certain
sense is subject to the same threat. Only the open society is in such a
danger, and that is the price that it pays for providing its citizens with
the freedom they desire. We must learn the technique of countering the
terrorists without losing that freedom.

Terrorism seems to be a movement as random as its selection of victims.
Yet there is now a reason to fear its consolidation. The conclusion all
points one way. For the first time perhaps terrorists have a base in a
well-established and powerful government. Terrorism for the Russians is not
only for home consumption but also for export. Yet in the Soviet Union
terrorists of many nations can find training schools and a source of money

and weapons.[12] Such a systematic arrangement is helping the social
revolution and therefore bringing on the millennium predicted for the ideal
of communism. As usual with such remote ideals, they result in the most
brutal and cowardly attacks.

   It is not sufficiently recognized that we are at war with the Soviet
Union. It is not yet a hot war fought with nuclear warheads and inter-
continental missles but it is no longer mild enough to be described as a
cold war. A warm war might be the nearest accurate description, for the
support of terrorists around the world, augmented by open and active aid to
revolutionaries in such countries as Nicaragua and Angola, can no longer be
described as peace. Without the aid and encouragement of the Soviet Union,
the terrorist movement would soon collapse. The extent of terrorism is a
measure of the aid provided by the Russians.

Notes

   1 William R. Corson and Robert T. Crowley, The New KGB:Engine of Soviet
Power (New York 1985, Morrow).
   2 Marvin E. Wolfgang and Franco Ferracuti, The Subculture of Violence
(London 1967, Tavistock Publications), pp. 202-205, 207, 208.
   3 For some of the material in this chapter I am greatly indebted to
Raynor's valuable book, Terrorism Past, Present and Future (New York
1982, Franklin Watts), to which I hereby hope I am making adequate as
well as grateful acknowledgement.
   4 New York Times, May 25, 1985, p. A-5.
   5 Ibid., August 18, 1985, p. 11
   6 From Hegel to Terrorism (New York 1985, Humanities Press),
chapter X.
   7 Karl Marx, Das Kapital (Berlin 1962, Dietz Verlag), p. 779.
   8 Op. cit., pp. 114-115.
   9 Op. cit., p. 120.
   10 The Boston Globe, July 15, 1985, p. 41.
   11 The New York Times, July 21, 1985, p. 1.
   12 Ray S. Cline and Yonah Alexander, Terrorism: The Soviet Connection
(New York 1984, Crane Russak).

Chapter 12

THE LIARS 1

There is every reason to include the Russians in a chapter of this
book. On a broad scale they have many times been terrorists, torturers,
murderers and massacrists — everything, in fact, in the line of
professional killers, with the single exception of cannibalism. This fact
is of course no new discovery. What is surprising, though, is that
Karl Marx himself warned the West of the dangers of Russian ambitions.

Between March 1853 and April 1956, Karl Marx wrote, in English, a series
of articles for the New York [Daily] Tribune.[1] This series, which was
devoted to the opinions of Czarist Russia, has never appeared either in
German or Russian, and for a good reason: it is a remarkable statement of
Marx's warning against Russian imperialism, and it shows by inference that
the rule of the masters of the Soviet Union is no different now from that
of their predecessors.

Marx was concerned with the expansonist tendencies of Russia and the
danger to the West. He saw in Russia the enemy of liberty and of the
European revolution.[2] Reports circulated by Russian agents, "that Russian
troops were marching to the frontier, that the Russian Consul at Galatz has
brought up an immense number of trees for the throwing of several bridges

across the Danube, and other <u>canards</u> ... are nothing but so many ridiculous attempts ... to strike a wholesome terror into the western world, and to push it to the continuance of that policy of extension, under the cover of which Russia hopes as heretofore, to carry out her projects upon the East".[3]

No one in charge of the Soviet Union wants it to be known that Marx, whose reputation as infallible has been carefully cultivated, was opposed to Russian ambitions, or that he regarded the struggle between capital and labor as second in importance to the antagonism between East and West, with his sympathies going entirely to the West. There was a consistent policy of Russian Czarist aggrandizement, which the Soviets have retained and cultivated. Communism is, in a word, Russian imperialism continued under another name. The present day communists have merely taken over the aims and ambitions of the Czars, and with another group of leaders endeavor to put them into effect. What we have, in sum, is the spectacle of an old imperialism engaged in spreading a new secular theology.

The Soviet Union as it is today was formed in all its essentials by Lenin during world war 1. Openly advocating and employing terror, Lenin made himself and a small group under his control the masters of Russia; terror was the instrument, with death the punishment for any infraction of his autocratic rule. No Czar had ever executed more individuals for deviation, no ruler had ever gathered into his own hands more power. And if in the end he became the victim of his own system, with Stalin replacing him, that did not alter what he had accomplished.

Humanism upside down, humanism in reverse; that was the achievement Lenin bequeathed to the Soviet state; terrorism replacing humanism in all the internal political relations of the Soviet Union. The ruthlessness, the brutality, the utter disregard for human life all are there in full measure; and there has been little change since Lenin put his principles and practices in place. It is an old kind of despotism, employed many times before by kings, emperors and absolute rulers generally, only this time clothed in the language and outlook of Marxism.[4]

I use the term 'Russian' rather than 'Soviet' in order to stress the continuity and the special racial relationship. For the present situation it would be easier to imagine what would have happened had there been no social revolution in Russia but instead the Czars and the other leaders of Imperial Russia had read, understood, and agreed with the works of Marx, Engels and Lenin, and strove to put their program into effect; for the policy currently followed is a mixture of old Russia and new Marxism. Many observers have noted the similarity between the old Imperial Russia of the Czars and the Soviet Union today: the same oppressive regime, the same secret police, the same anti-Semitism, the same nationalism, the same foreign wars. The Soviet Union is simply the old Czarist regime under a fresh set of masters and a different political philosophy. The slogans are new but the game is not.

What could be more ironic than the fact that the Russians, from Bakunin and the anarchists who were against all governments, to Marx and the communists, should end by establishing the most repressive of regimes? There was something of the anarchist about Marx, too: his violent revolution was supposed to end by establishing a classless society and one without a government; and if he felt the final issue unresolved because he neglected to specify what the ideal was finally to be, it was no accident but the result of a deliberate belief that no government was necessary. Man, as Rousseau had averred, is essentially good if left to his own devices, and needs no laws or overseers to make him do the right thing. In the meanwhile, and without date, the dictatorship of the proletariat was intended to be a necessary stage on the way in the inevitable march of the dialectic.

But when, one might ask, have men who were in possession of absolute power ever been known to relinquish it? The Russian masses are never consulted and rarely even informed. Therefore those in the government feel no need to be consistent or even to be faithful to their own stated ideals. The New Soviet Constitution, promulgated in a third draft in 1936, promised an independent judicial system, freedom of religious worship, freedom of speech and freedom of the press, all freedoms which have been mocked in practice.

The Russians had not the slightest intention of adhering to the articles of the Helsinki Accord, and when some of their own citizens endeavored to monitor compliance, they were arrested and sent either to internal exile in Siberia or to "treatment" in mental hospitals. "Internal exile" —— what an admission that is! That conditions are so bad in parts of the Soviet Union and allowed to remain that way, that it is punishment enough just to be sent there to live!

The Helsinki Accord of 1975 was the work of President Carter, who had a special interest in human rights. Under Principle Seven, the Soviet government along with the other signatories, undertook to "respect human rights and fundamental freedoms". The Russians went along and clearly signed an agreement they had no intention of keeping. Worse: it brought dissenters out into the open where they could be caught and punished, another instance of deliberate deception on the part of the Soviet government.[5] Thus the Helsinki Accords "actually increased the volume and ferocity of human rights violations in Soviet Russia".

Many a pact has been signed with the cynical Russians, who hope that the other signatories will adhere to it while they have no such intention, an arrangement which provides them with an obvious advantage. They also practice a systematic and transparent deception when they accuse others of doing exactly what they are doing, thus attempting to disarm criticism in advance, a technique which unfortunately often works only too well.

Worse of all, perhaps, is the practice of "disinformation", a polite term for deliberate lies which they tell to their advantage. The spread of lies in order to mislead their enemies in the free world is considered of suffi- cient strategic importance in the Soviet Union to have it assigned a separate department. Our information comes partly from a Soviet defector.[6] Set up in 1959 and provided with ample funds as a separate operation with the KGB, the often skillful dissemination of falsehoods has met with considerable success even though it has its share of clumsy efforts.

Lest anyone think that Russian disinformation is directed only at their enemies, one needs only to consider their predilection for rewriting history to suit their own purposes, aimed at their own people. The biographies which are issued officially of past and present leaders in the Kremlin revise history to make it conform to such supposed facts as would flatter the position of the current supreme leader. It was true of Khrushchev, it was true of Brezhnev, and no doubt in time it will be true also of Gorbachev. History is made to become what the lackeys of the leaders say it is.

The practice of lying is so outrageously bad that a prominent literary figure much in favor at home has felt compelled to come out against it. In a speech to the Union of Soviet Writers, the poet Yevgeny Yevtushenko criticized the rewriting of events to suit political goals, official silence on such things as purges and peasant exterminations, and the discarding of once-prominent figures no longer in favor.[7]

Indeed in the way of deception in the effort to destablize the West, there is nothing the Russians consider too mean, dirty or despicable, as witness for example the letters sent to black American athletes who were proposing to take part in the Olympics of 1984 in Los Angeles, threatening letters purporting to have come from members of the Ku Klux Klan but so badly done that the forgeries were obvious.

The same can be noted about the class struggle which the Russians, following Marx, made so much of, for the class distinction has been reintroduced by the emergence of a privileged class, moreover one which is not acknowledged openly but catered to regularly.[8] The use of country houses: (dachas), of large chauffered limousines; of special restaurants and shops reserved to them; of apartments with live-in maids; of privately delivered and unmarked envelopes filled with cash: the party packet system, called pay for the "thirteenth month" and the "Kremlin ration", of private tutors and special schools; is evidence of the existence of favored and privileged classes, of which, according to Mr. Willis, there are five, all higher than the urban and rural working classes: a top class, a military class, and a triple-layered rising class. The nomenklatura system is an actual listing of the state-registered Soviet elite. There are still other benefits: better housing, cultural concerts, holiday facilities and even foreign travel, all aided by "blat", i.e. the use of personal contracts and of bribery to make the ordinary conditions of life more bearable.

In short, the Russians have subordinated their Marxist ideal of communism to their own special interests whenever it has suited them to do so. They are faithful to nothing unless they stand to gain from it. The revolution has changed both the character and the personnel of the aristo-cracy but did not eliminate the need for one, and will not until the day when no group is more intelligent and powerful than any other. It is the largest and most ruthless dictatorship going. The Politburo exercises a total and absolute control, interfering in the slightest affair when it sees fit or has something at stake. For there are no effective laws in the Soviet Union. It is a government of men, not of laws; the law is whatever the Politburo decides, for the government is a party to every legal transaction. That has been true ever since Stalin's mass extermination of the millions of small farmers, the "kulaks", in the early 1930s.

Admittedly, there is only one human species to which everybody belongs, but cultural determination is very strong and makes all the difference, particularly if it has survived for a number of generations. This is the case with the Russians. Most Russians until the communist revolution were serfs, and serfdom is a particularly brutalizing way of life. The ancestors of the present-day ruling class were in all likelihood serfs, and the reckless disregard of life that is portrayed in all accounts of serfdom is no doubt continued by their descendents, who have never known any other scale of values.

The rigid autocracy of the Politburo together with the military and the secret service continues that tradition. Defections from the KGB and from the military intelligence (the GRU) are treated in an especially brutal fashion. Betrayal exacts a terrible death, so everyone suspects and spies on everyone else.[9] Unfortunately, in any large-scale struggle, the cruelest and most ruthless regime has a temporary advantage over those with respect for human life and laws, but such a regime must fail in the end because it has no stability of social organization, only a reign of terror. In the meanwhile, of course, it can be immensely destructive.

As we saw in chapter XI, one institution, and a very significant one, was taken over by the Soviets from the reign of the Czars and greatly expanded: the secret police, called the Okhrana. The successor to the Okhrana was the KGB, now second in size only to the armed forces and probably superior to them in power in the Russian state, according to some informed opinion even secretly ruling over the state. Occasionally the power struggle surfaces briefly, as when in the Kremlin Beria was murdered. One thing is sure: the public is never told of how the changes are made or what transpires in the highest reaches of the Russian government, no more so now than when the Czarist nobility was in power.

There are currently not enough farmers to work the land sufficiently to feed the country, and much grain has to be imported. Too many men have been siphoned off for the army and the KGB. The economic insufficiency indicated an emphasis on military might and on secret terror that can never provide the kind of morale that makes a country great. Repression and destruction is not a solid basis but it is the only one that can be built by thugs and spies, the heirs and assigns of Felix Dzerzhinsky, as the only method of rule he had learned from his Czarist masters.

It is not sufficiently recognized that the Russians are racists. The Politburo does not possess a single oriental face, and this despite the enormous populations of Mongolian peoples. There is a quiet but determined effort to replace Marx, the half-Jewish German, with Nicolai Lenin, the Russian, despite the obvious fact that it was Marx who initiated the movement. The Russians are anti-Semites still, and indeed anti-foreigners.

This mean and bigoted people as it happens have been handed by circumstances an enormous opportunity. The British Empire declined with two world wars, and the only other large power, the United States, has no territorial ambitions. The Russians are in a position ot move into great power status which they are obviously endeavoring to do.

The British Empire in the 18th and 19th centuries was the largest the world has ever seen. It included more territory and more people than any before it. Ships and railways furnished the technology that had made it all possible. However, the Boer War in South Africa 1899-1902 marked the turn, and two world wars weakened the British hold on the rest of the world. The arrival of the airplane took away the British advantage, for that invention made it possible to penetrate the military barrier the British navy had furnished. The development of world-wide communication as well as transportation did the rest.

What has gone with the modern world of the 1920s to 1980s is the rule of law and with it all respect for the individual's right to his life. Nations large and small have learned to live on opportunism in the hands of the few self-perpetuating politicians. With the rule of law went justice, equality, all the old standards and values. Their place was taken by brute force, and the name of the new game was politics, unrestricted, to replace economics and indeed all other human relations by the military.

The ebbing of the British Empire, all of it from India to South Africa, left a vacuum. The only other world-class power, the United States, had no inclination to fill it, for with its vast continent it had no need of more land. There had been a great influx of immigrants following the Civil War, hence no need of more people, either.

The vacuum, then, still exists, and the only power anxious to fill it is the Soviet Union. The Marxist philosophy, which emphasized not nations but economic classes, furnished the motive, and it was not long after the Russian Revolution that its leaders began to think in terms of world conquest. But where the British tried to establish by force the rule of law, the Russians try to establish by force only the rule of force. All of

138

the virtues of civilization, such as respect for human life, tolerance of
difference, forbearance, brotherly love, are absent.

I cannot conclude a chapter on the Soviet Union as professional liars
without a reference to the deliberate abuse of psychiatry. Here the
evidence is very clear, and it has been recorded: the Russians classify as
mentally ill all political dissidents. To criticize the Soviet government
in any way is taken as hard evidence of schizophrenia and so the critic is
confined to a mental hospital and treated accordingly. The treatment seems
more designed to punish than to cure, consisting in the use of physical
torture as well as the excessive administration of drugs.

Observers in the west well qualified to judge came to the considered
judgment that psychiatrists in the Soviet Union were behaving as agents of
the secret police, the KGB.

All of this came to a head when it became clear that the World
Psychiatric Association (the WPA) was about to expel the Soviets: accordingly,
the All-Union Society of Psychiatrists and Neurologists announced in
February 1983 that it was withdrawing from that body.[10] This was as clear
a confession of guilt as it was possible to make. It was also a cynical
admission that the Russians had no intention of mending their ways in this
regard.

There could be no greater perversion of the truth than the assumption
that dissidents are mentally ill and that therefore conformity is equivalent
to sanity. Lies are officially defended as truths and the liars rewarded
by those supreme politicians who dictate and control all thought and
expression.

The psychology of the Russians is very unlike our way of thinking. The
taking of human life, even on a wholesale scale, is not on anyone's

conscience; there is no respect for human life as such. The behavior of those in charge of the invasion and subjugation of Afghanistan is evidence enough.[11] The invasion began in 1979 and it is still in progress, guided by a deliberate policy of extermination of all those who will not accept Soviet rule.

The essential unity of the methods of Hitler and Stalin proved that the Soviet Union is a fascist state. Substitute 'class' for 'race' and you have the true parallel. The socialism of Marx and Engels was after all only a verbal front, intended to disguise and conceal the ruthless dictatorship that Stalin had learned from Hitler and that has been the method of all subsequent leaders in the Soviet Union, including the Politbureau itself.

The success of the Russians in getting hold of a large country and manipulating its people at will has not mellowed the Soviet leadership. Indeed just the opposite is true, for the aim now is world domination. There is no way in which the military action of the Russians in Angola, Cuba, Granada, and El Salvador can be called defensive, for they are nowhere near the borders of the Soviet Union. One country that is, Afghanistan, with its poorly developed culture, could hardly have been regarded as a threat to the Russians who beginning in December 1979 have brought all the might of a full military arsenal: tanks, bombers and gun ships, and wave after wave of mechanized infantry, against an opponent who is attempting to defend his own country with rifles. The United States evinced only a negative interest in this enterprise. She had no ambition to dominate but only a negative one: the United States could not allow the Soviet Union to do so in a world as small as the rapid progress in communication and transportation have made it.

It became therefore a matter of survival, and it remains one. The

United States is in the awkward position of not wanting to rule the world but also of not allowing the Soviet Union to do so. This brought the two nations into the conflict that prevails today and that has begun to rub at the edges where their interests meet, for instance in Angola, in Nicaragua, and indeed everywhere there is Soviet expansion.

Notes

1 Marx vs. Russia, J. A. Doerig, ed., Afterword by Hans Kohn (New York 1962, Frederick Ungar Publishing Co.), p. 11.

2 Marx vs. Russia, J. A. Doerig, ed., (New York 1962, Frederick Ungar Publishing Co.).

3· Ibid., p. 19.

4 See e. g. Paul Johnson, Modern Times (New York 1983, Harper & Row), especially pp. 66-71.

5 See e. g. Paul Johnson, Modern Times (Harper & Row, 1983) pp. 277, 673, 680.

6 Ladislav Bittman, The KGB and Soviet Disinformation: An Insider's View (New York 1985, Pergamon-Brassey). See also the report on the Soviet Campaign of Disinformation in the Congressional Record for October 17, 1985, Volume 131, E 4662-to E 4666.

7 Associated Press dispatch for December 19, 1985.

8 Mervyn Matthews, Privilege in The Soviet Union (London 1978, George Allen & Unwin); Michael Voslensky, Nomenklatura (London 1984, The Bodley Head; David K. Willis, Klass (New York 1985, St. Martin's Press); Bohdan Harasymiw, Political Elite Recruitment in the Soviet Union (Oxford 1985, University Press).

9 Viktor Surorov, Aquarium (London 1985, Hamish Hamilton); also N. Shevchenko, Breaking with Moscow (London 1985, Cape).

10 Eric Stover and Elena O. Nightingale, The Breaking of Bodies and Minds (New York 1985, W. H. Freeman). The whole of Part 2 of this book, which was sponsored by the American Association for the Advancement of Science (the AAAS), is devoted to an account of psychiatric abuse in the Soviet Union.

11 Edward R. Girardet, Afghanistan: The Soviet War (New York 1986, St. Martin's Press).

Chapter 13

THE LIARS 2

The struggle for freedom and against tyranny and oppression has led to
a series of national defeats in recent decades. Communism represents a
kind of step backward to the kind of rigid control against which all free
people have always fought. One can only hope that it will not last. After
all, the Berlin wall was constructed to keep East Germans in, not to keep
West Germans out. How many people would there be in Cuba, Poland, or even
in the Soviet Union, for that matter, if emigration was freely permitted?
Rigid border controls are all that stand in the way of a mass exodus. The
leaders of the communists, Gorbachev, Castro, and the others, would not dare
open their borders, for they know if they did their countries would be
emptied in a short while.

Quincy Wright has tried to show that socialism always leads to war, and
he has some good precedents to cite in defense of that statement: ancient
Assyria and classic Sparta, as well as early Peru and the pre-world war 2
governments of Italy, Germany, Russia and Japan.[1] Any war with the current
nuclear weapons must be one that nobody wins, but it will be hard to
convince the Russian leadership of that.

Perhaps the Russian ambition to conquer the world is within reach, if only one obstacle can be overcome. The United States alone stand in the way, and therefore must be eliminated. The entire effort of the Soviet Union at the present time is the defeat of the United States in one way or another.

The Russians have available to them a weapon whose awesome power has not been recognized. It is not exactly a secret but it is one currently under-estimated and overlooked by the Americans. That weapon is philosophy. I mean of course one particular systematic philosophy: the writings of Marx, Engels and Lenin as the application of that philosophy both in theory and practice.

The innocent but insidious work of pragmatism, as understood by William James (as distinct from that of C. S. Peirce), has conformed well to a frontier society that has so much country to open up and so many material resources that it could turn its back on theory and get on with the work of developing the land. The result is that while a philosophy has been taught to every school child in the Soviet Union as a creed to live by, the United States has gone the other way and assumed that its tremendous technical development backed by the theory and practice of the scientific method in the physical sciences needs no philosophy, which is thereby relegated to the back pages of history along with alchemy and astrology. Thus while the history of philosophy is flourishing in the universities as a humanities alternative, those who run the country's government, business and industry have no conception of what philosophy really is or what its social power might be. We have therefore nothing with which to counter the Russian threat on the propaganda front.

Nothing, it seems, ever goes altogether right. The philosophers in Europe and the United States tend to ignore not only Marx but with him all materialism. The western philosophers in rejecting Marxism rejected also

all versions of materialism. This means of course also rejecting the
philosophy of scientific materialism which agrees with Aristotle's
conception of matter —— not Feuerbach's —— and still has considerable
validity. Aristotle envisaged a matter containing forms, and the forms as
possibilities which to that extent can have their being apart from matter.

Unfortunately, the Marxist interpret matter only in terms of the class
struggle, and ignore the achievements of the middle class, which are many:
democracy, liberalism, individual freedom, the physical sciences, together
with technology, large-scale industrial production and scientific agriculture. The Marxists encourage the use of violence to achieve the kind of
society they find desirable. Indeed the general Marxists' position is to
justify the use of terrorism, torture, murder, and even massacre as well as
urban guerilla violence because they think it leads to the proletarian social
revolution.

The Russians have learned how to employ a metaphysics as an instrument of
policy. For the first time perhaps a philosophy has been used explicitly to
direct a society, an effort deflected, however, by nationalism and racism,
which have the effect of rendering it more brutal and uncompromising.

There is no power in social life greater than a system of ideas when it
is associated with the name of a compelling person. In the past this has
usually come from a religious institution, as with Moses, Jesus, Mohammad,
but it could issue from any other. The latest version is from political
economy, and is called by the name of Marx.

It may be in the end nothing less than a philosophy, with its metaphysical theory of what is real, that will tip the balance in the struggle
between East and West. In that struggle, alas, the West is not even aware
of what is involved, innocent of the power of abstract ideas in the power

struggle between peoples, an ignorance which renders vulnerable those who must compete for the minds and hence the wills of others.

The Russian combination of military might with abstract ideas is awesome to contemplate. The new Marxist imperialism of the Soviet Union is powered by a philosophy, that most potent of forces. How then can we oppose it without having one ourselves? That is the question. The Russians are known to have an arsenal second to none, and they have the philosophy constructed by Marx, Engels, and Lenin. Never has destruction been planned on such a massive scale. The deliberate preparation for world conquest requires the largest of dimensions. The United States also has a large military establishment, but one intended for defensive purposes also.

Taken by itself, war is by long odds the most destructive activity ever engaged in by the human species. The aim of war is the elimination of the enemy, and that is entirely negative. There are exceptions, however, wars which have cleared the way for constructive after-effects. The wars conducted by Alexander the Great throughout most of his short life (356-323 BC), has the positive result of spreading Greek culture and thus of preserving it for future generations. The British Empire in the eighteenth and nineteenth centuries also left positive effects: the spread of common law, parliamentary democracy, railroads, civil service, and a common language.

Now what broad culture could the Russians offer assuming that they conquered the world? They have added little or nothing, they have only expanded the repressive side of the previous Czarist regime; they have greatly expanded the secret police and the armed forces, nothing else.

> "The evil of Russia is not the impulse to economic
> reform [but] its inhumane and historically inadequate
> political method, absolutism....Russian political

> absolutism currently fails to provide the moral
> atmosphere necessary for free intellectual
> enterprise....Russia borrows easily the West's
> technology, but does she borrow the moral culture
> out of which true scientific innovation grows?"[2]

The sole plus in the Russian picture is the development of the physical

sciences and the educational process to cultivate it.[3] But that does not

include the social sciences, which would require an impartial view of social

organization, which the Russians could not tolerate.

The religious horrors of the Christian Middle Ages are being continued

in the modern world by the Moslem fundamentalists, and now they have been

joined by the secular horrors of the Marxists, Russian style. The Russians

are supported in their actions by their absolute belief. The fact is that

Marxism has not been widely recognized as the religious movement that it is.

It has all the fervor and demands all the adherence of total commitment.

The Marxist secular religion parallels the Christian in many respects:

Marx corresponds to God, Engels to Jesus and Lenin the Holy Ghost, with

Stalin the St. Paul, of the movement. This atheistic pantheon is taught in

all the schools in the Soviet Union, though of course the explicitly

religious aspect is not.

There is of course the ever-present enemy called capitalism but

including with it democracy, individualism, human rights, freedom. Marxism

is despotism under a new banner, and equipped with the half-truth of

materialism in Feuerbach's older and out-dated version. In the last

century physicists have discovered many new properties of matter and the

technologists have devised many new uses for it that engineers apply. That

makes the older version on which the Russians rely obsolete. They have not

noticed the contradiction. For our part we have not noticed that the half-

truth of the older materialism is also half true.

Lenin did not teach that "those who are not with us are against us", he taught instead that "those who are not with us must be killed", and the Russians have been practicing that precept ever since. Marxism has the same ideal force of any new religion, for ideas always have been and remain the most potent weapons. Remember that Christianity conquered the Roman Empire without using the sword. When the Emperor Constantine in AD 324 became the sole ruler, he proclaimed Christianity to be the official truth, though he was baptized only on his deathbed. His conversion was almost surely for political reasons.

Now that transportation and communication have become world-wide, someone always dreams of global domination. First it was Hitler, and now the Russians; only this time instead of an individual it is a committee ambition, which is more dangerous; and more dangerous also because justified by an all-enveloping philosophy. Even so there is reason to doubt that the world is ready for it, so that all the effort will produce is the cataclysm of a nuclear war.

Peace in such terms is only a rest stop engaged in when men temporarily grow weary of fighting. Ideas are simply conflicts at the intellectual level. This was true of the ancient Greeks for all their wide-ranging cultural achievements, and it is still true today. We have learned nothing except how to develop more efficient weapons.

The Russian pretension of serving as the dedicated international leaders of communism is being gradually stripped away. What motivates the Soviets is not communism but nationalism -- the nationalism of the Russians, who do not hesitate to deceive their enemies into thinking that they are the dis-passionate advocates of a position they hold is best for everybody. Nationalist Russia is the inheritor of Imperial Russia; not the Russia of the much heralded classless society but the Russia of the new priviliged classes whose leadership, as we have noted, the master of the Kremlin sedulously maintains.

Nationalism is a more potent force than is generally recognized. It takes from two to three generations to assimilate to another culture. Nothing cuts deeper than nationalism, and for a very good reason: it is the set of ideas that an individual absorbs from his or her birth onward without knowing that such a process exists. The United States has developed a culture of its own which affects those who are born within its borders, regardless of their original ethnic or cultural origins. In the hands of the Russians, armed with an absolute philosophy, the state has become an overwhelming and paralyzing force, more constrictive than facilitative, and, very much like the Nazis and Fascists, organized for war.

The Russians are nationalists who have risked everything on world conquest. They cannot point to any other achievement in the meanwhile. They have never gone through the Renaissance, never experienced the softening effects of that tradition, never known that the aim of good will was to help others to live less painful lives. They have never participated in the humanist revolution in which the western nations of Europe all took part; they have never regarded human life, individual human life, as of any value, and have never thought in terms of sympathy, pity, friendship, altruism, fairness, reason, and the like, sentiments which have made life worth while for so many in Italy, France, England, Holland, Belgium, and Germany. They have never been educated in the works of Locke, Montesquieu, Rousseau, and the many others who turned civilization into a tolerant affair.

They can boast, perhaps, of a complacent population but certainly not of a happy or prosperous one. Victory or defeat in war is what the

Russians are facing. Their entire effect has been and continues to be entirely negative. That is why they have earned a place in a book devoted to the underside of human nature. The Russians must take their place among the destroyers.

From ground level, where facing the Russians our choice seems to be fight or become slaves, there seems little to debate: we wish to remain free even if it means dying. Facing the Russians, Betrand Russell decided he would rather be a communist than a casualty: "better red than dead"; but that would not be everyone's choice. What it would be is up to us to decide, always providing of course than the course of events does not make the decision for us.

Notes

1 Op. cit., p. 305 ff.
2 Weston La Barre, The Human Animal (Chicago, University Press, 1954), pp. 227-228.
3 See e. g. Scientific Education in Mongolia Nature, 311, 97 (1984).

Chapter 14

THE PROBLEM

Despite the divisions indicated by the various chapters of this book,
it consists in a single argument. All those who have taken the low road to
the underside of human nature belong in the same group. For terrorists can
also be torturers, murderers can become massacrists, absolute believers can
resort to war.

For, as we have noted, the fact is that people everywhere come in the
same variety. Societies large and small, primitive or advanced, all
exhibit the same broad spectrum of individuals having advantages and short-
comings, with at one end the feeble-minded and criminally bent and at the
other the talented and well-intentioned, the largest proportion being in
the middle. Which group rises to the surface and takes charge of the
others depends on many factors, certainly on circumstances to some extent.
Thus the most able might use the system to run the society most efficiently,
as has happened in the United States, or the criminally insane may gain
control and lead the society to its ruin, as happened in Nazi Germany.

One might think that the term, crime, applies here but it does not. As
two authorities explain, some acts are regarded as crimes by all societies:

murder, theft, robbery and incest; whereas others, such as homosexuality, bribery, embezzlement, extortion and fraud, are not.[1] Moreover, the state always appropriated to itself acts which are not permitted to individual citizens: execution, castration, torture, incarceration, and many more.

Although all social events take place in broad view of the public, the direction of a society is determined by so many variables that its outcome is at present unpredictable. There are some forces which for the moment have not been recognized but which influence the outcome. Obviously, society is the result of the sum of the individuals and organizations composing it, but the mechanism is complex and for the present not understood sufficiently to make predictions possible.

Those like Mahatma Gandhi and Konrad Lorentz who believed in the ultimate victory of truth are forgetting that in the material world there are no absolutes.[2] The error of the action of idealists is to suppose that there are. The ideal is by definition unattainable. No wonder, then, that so many profess one philosophy while following another.

Perhaps the point can be made best by contrasting hatred with love. Hatred has to end with extinction; if the object of hate is murder, there is nothing left to hate. By contrast, love is so pervasive that its actions get lost. Either way, the emotions serve as poor guides to behavior; they are so common, the intellect so rare. Yet the fact is that those who are responsible for their actions are more swayed by emotions than by reason; more appealed to by relatives; more attracted to high promises than to modest ones; more influenced by bad news than by good.

In the early chapters of this study I have tried to show how much that is reprehensible in life was laid down early. It might be illuminating to note that human nature was formed against a background of non-human nature, and that nature, in a word, can be cruel. We see this in the death of those young whose end is brought on by painful cancer. For those who survive enemies and accidents, there await old age, disasters, disintegration and death. In short, when men exercise aggression against other men, they are only expressing one aspect of nature. Natural occurrences, such as earth-quakes, volcanic eruptions, tsunami, and the like, generally destroy or maim human individuals impartially. Innocence or guilt plays no part; the pain and destruction are the same. We saw this in the earthquake that hit Mexico City in 1986 and the volcanic eruption and mud slide in Panama in the same year.

Every special group, whether large or small, whether because of a common religion or because of a common politics or philosophy, seems committed to compelling others to accept the same set of beliefs, or die. Until men and women can give up the idea of killing those who do not share their faith, there can be little hope for the human species and no reason to see it preserved. And until we learn how to put the interests of a common humanity above all lesser loyalties, whether of tribe, religion or nation, there can be no hope for mankind. Unfortunately, the evidence is against our achieving such a goal, and so as we become more efficient with our techno-logy there is the danger that me might utterly destroy ourselves.

There is no such thing as man born into a conventional state of nature; all infants are information receptors; though there is no inborn political system and no inherent morality, all remains to be learned. Since societies vary widely, this means that there is no native way of behaving other than what a given society imposes and requires. Infants of all species learn from their parents by imitation what is expected of them, and this is no less true of the human species. There is no such thing as a uniformly human way of doing things, only those of the tribe, the group, the nation or the state. Under this rubric, differences are bound to appear and become the subject of conflict. Warring groups of the same species do not exist in any other species. The practice is inherently human and of course makes for immense difficulties.

The collective, whatever the size and shape it takes, has the responsibility of directing the individuals composing it, and can turn them either into members of a co-operative unit or into adversaries geared for aggression. Peace or war; that is the choice of the collective, and it almost always lies beyond the control of the single individual.

The power of cultural determination is the strongest of all social forces. We will need to recognize this if we wish to understand the Nazi holocaust or the Russians of today in Afghanistan. The German Nazis and the Russian communists are in themselves convincing evidence that nothing lies ahead of us but war and destruction. It would probably require something as radical as a mutation of the human species to achieve anything like the brotherhood of man. In the meanwhile anyone who has made himself familiar with the atrocities committed in the last half century must be, to some extent, at least, ashamed to be human.

World theories, such as Marxism, are not accepted for their truth but for their appeal. Here seems to be the justification for any group which wants to seize power and possessions from those already entrenched in an older system. The have-nots can claim that history is on their side, by which they mean that the proof of the rightness of their cause will consist in winning.

It is possible therefore that we will live to see the triumph of a form of government which, wherever it succeeds, immediately cancels all individual values and freedoms in favor of an absolute conformity, with penalties for infractions consisting in torture and death. Perhaps the results of a nuclear war with the Soviet Union will change all the social forecasts. It is too early to say, though currently the signs are not good.

Can an open society, such as exists in the United States survive and triumph over a totally-controlled one, such as the USSR? This is the number one question of our time, and it will determine the future for many generations. The information needed in order to answer this question is there but it has not been properly assembled, and so we are left in some doubt.

What is one to conclude, however, from the thesis that man is essentially a killer? How plan for a peaceful world, for the long-range construction of useful artifacts and the pursuit of humanitarian aims?

This study was undertaken in the hope that if mankind were confronted with the facts, there might be hope for a change; and any change would have to be for the better.

Ecology, the study of the relationships of organisms to their environment, has its human counterpart in the study of the relationships of societies to their artificial environment, and this is no less true because the societies have shaped that environment in response to organic needs. Unfortunately, these responses take into account only the needs of individuals in a given society, not of all living individuals in all societies. The result is that paradoxically what is achieved by one society, if it happens to be more productive than others, is to create an imbalance between societies, and that generates competition and, finally, that largest and most intense of competitions: war.

All studies of human motivation seem to assume that the human organism is a closed system and that all aims and efforts must be studied within it. But the fact is that human conduct must be understood as a set of responses to other individuals and to artifacts. If you want to produce a certain kind of social behavior, then see to it that there is a proper sort of back-ground, for the organ-artifact circuit is all-determining.

Given this situation, then, the task is to learn what kind of stimulus will bring about responses that call for less destructive aggression. Violence is not unprovoked, but the provocations are not always easy to locate on the spectrum of motivations. This, then, is the remedy. Tell me what kind of society you want and I will tell you two ways to bring it about.

The first way is genetic. By altering the genetic inheritance it ought to be possible to produce desirable changes in behavior. Lumsden and Wilson have suggested how this may be accomplished, with a reduction in destructive behavior in favor of constructive.[3]

The second way is cultural. All animals survive by adapting to their environment, and this is no less true of man. Now, however, he has a new environment: the cultural environment he has built for himself. He made it, and he can alter it. By producing the kind of artificial environment that would be most conducive to a peaceful and constructive society, humanity can arrange for its own better future. Heredity thus will have its effects, but these will be controlled by the environment which is in a position to select those traits it wants and eliminate those it finds obstructive.

This is the program suggested by scientific materialism.

Marxism is not scientific, its "dialectical materialism" is not scientific materialism. Its Hegelian basis in metaphysics works in the wrong direction: not down from the largest assumptions but up from the smallest. The Marxists have been allowed to preempt materialism, as

though theirs was the only kind. The physical sciences, and in particular
biology, has another one to offer. The minimal assumptions must issue from
the work of the neurophysiologists, not from dogmatists.

A basic change in human nature which could take place without the loss of
constructive aggression could be accomplished by eliminating all aggression
that is destructive. At the present time we have no knowledge of how this
could be done.

Social energy must be redirected into productive channels of peaceful
competition. The true materialists are those who produce prosperity by
means of increased agricultural yield, manufacture and trade. This has been
true of western Europe, the United States and Japan. The Marxist countries,
led by the Soviet Union, have been responsible for nothing but war and
revolution and a decreased production. Russia before the communists was a
net exporter of grain; since the revolution she has become a large importer.
The contrast between the standard of living of the Soviet bloc of nations
and the western alliance speaks for itself.

There is one final principle which we had better face even though it
represents a counsel of despair.

Every positive attraction has an implied exclusion clause.

This is, alas, true of religious faith, romantic love, patriotism, or
any other kind of absolute commitment. An absolute belief that carries no
such clause is impossible of attainment; to be dedicated to X, whatever X
may be means to set it in opposition to Y, Z, etc. The implied exclusion
clause is entirely negative, and even though it is unstated it is still
effective.

In the implied exclusion clause we can locate the seeds of human
aggression. The positive, however firmly seated, has its negative effects.

To choose this, whatever it may be, is by the same logic to not-choose that. Every choice is an affront to the not chosen. Thus we may expect conflict to continue to be a fact of life. We can try to hold down all destructive activities: the aggressive behavior of cannibals, warriors, slavers, massacrists, murderers, torturers, terrorists and liars; but we cannot expect to eliminate them altogether.

The ideal, of course, would be to discover social laws as fundamental to human existence as the natural laws of the physical sciences are, in a word, social laws which are also natural and which are to be found in that unbroken chain of levels which runs up from the physical to the cultural.

At the cultural level there is a startling monotony in the successive waves of civilizations and barbarians. As soon as the barbarians become civilized, they in their turn become the victims of later barbarians. The Roman barbarians, for example, conquered the civilized Athenians, and then centuries after the Romans became civilized, they themselves were conquered by the barbarian German Goths.

All barbarians take easily to absolute belief, and always see it in terms of violent application. The Gothic conquerors of the Roman Empire took to a simplified version of Christianity which they supported with force. The modern parallel is the Soviets' version of Marxism, which they apply with utter ruthlessness. The Soviets evidently think they can acquire European civilization through conquest, and they wait patiently now for the opportunity to do so. If they succeed in destroying Europe in the process, they will have the task of recovering culture from the ruins, as the Romans recovered Greek culture from their educated Greek slaves. Hegel thought that those who were ignorant of history would be compelled to repeat it, but those who are familiar with it seem to be under the same compulsion.

I have tried to show in the chapter on absolute belief (chapter 6) that we can anticipate no relief from it but that if continued to be left to govern the human species this time it may prove fatal. Although most populations have increased exponentially in recent centuries, so has the efficiency of weapons of destruction. There is no survival down that road; indeed there can be none unless we learn how to substitute moderate belief for absolute belief, how to be able to act, in other words, from beliefs which offer little more than half conviction.

The lesson of history is that people on the whole can live with any kind of social order in preference to chaos, and nihilism of whatever variety eventually leads to chaos. Establishing an order is a long slow process, and often comes only after a period of turmoil, for these things have their rhythm even though it is imperfectly understood. There are absolutes for this, too, but they can promise only temporary relief. What is sorely needed at this state is a set of moderate beliefs promising elasticity of adherence.

The only lasting remedy known to mankind for the killer instinct is the rule of law. A good example is to be found in British India (1783-1947) from the taking over of the East India Company to Independence, and we may look at it for a moment for the lesson it affords. When the Moghul Empire fell apart and the last Moghul was peacefully deposed by the British, "the people of India submitted to British rule because it was infinitely better than that which obtained in India at the end of the last century" [i.e. the 18th].[4]

I am not here condoning the many monstrous errors committed by the British in India, including the racial distinction which left all Indians as second-class citizens in their own country. I am only using as good

examples the many benefits. These can be seen best in what the Indians
retained. The British was the only power ever to have ruled over all of
India. After Independence some of the benefits of British rule were kept
by the Indians as indispensable: the railways, the army, the civil service,
the legal system, parliamentary democracy, and even the English language.

The rule of law is a clear example of mankind restraining itself,
turning all the exercise of violent aggression over to the state. Of course
there has been state-ordered violence, from which the British in India were
not exempt, after the Mutiny, for example; but on the whole the British
performed the best service when they themselves submitted to the rule of
law.

In a properly ordered society, altruism would be unnecessary, for the
minimum provisions necessary to sustain the less advantaged individuals
would be in place. That has not been the situation at any time before the
present so far as our records go. It is obviously an ideal at which to
aim; with altruism and the generosity of individuals only a stop gap.
Spontaneous altruism meanwhile measures the extent of a common human
sympathy and the feeling of a kinship with all the members of the species.
Individuals who risk their lives to save the lives of total strangers occur
somewhere almost daily and usually by individuals who think they deserve no
special reward. When official societies are organized and their intentions
codified, no provision is ever made for this side of human nature.

Of course the rule of law can be misused, as for instance when governments become severely restrictive rather than merely regulative and
facilitative, which, alas, is usually the case; or when nation-states
extend their control by force beyond their own borders. What is needed to
save mankind from becoming a victim of its own destructive violence is to

extend the rule of law as practiced in Great Britain and the United States voluntarily to the entire surface of the globe, though not necessarily under any particular aegis but rather by general agreement. How this is to be accomplished we have yet to discover, and for the moment the only contender for world government is the Soviet Union, as clear an advocate of violent conquest as ever existed. But a global rule of law cannot be established by any nation-state employing force. If it is to be based on moderate rather than absolute belief, it must be introduced by common consent.

The point is that moderate beliefs call for tentative actions, and tentative actions are not irreversible: they can be modified or even changed if reason and fact together indicate that it would be wise that they should. Proceed cautiously and without total conviction, that is the guidance that is called for. It is admittedly a learned behavior, and will not come easily.

At the end of sanity there awaits for those who are able to cope with it a method of construction that has no equal: the scientific method of investigation, with its accompanying technology. To this alternative, then, we must turn our final attention.

Fortunately, this method is known: the experimental method of investigation as practiced by the physical scientists. It begins with observation and experiment, moves to the formation of hypotheses, then, before any application can be tried, tests the hypotheses for truth or falsity by means of experiment and calculation. An hypothesis in this sense is a universal proposition that might just be true and is therefore up for examination. If false, it is abandoned and another one tested, until some measure of success is achieved.

The most basic tenet of science is that no law however firmly established is absolute; and may be abandoned if the evidence against it calls for such action.

At once of course I must admit that, with the suggestion that the method of the physical sciences be applied to the case of absolute social belief, there is a serious problem, for the method is in the physical area and the suggestion in the social area. Given the integrative levels in nature, such that the physical is the name for the lower levels and the social for the higher and more complex, it follows that the social area must contain many more variables than we have yet learned how to deal with adequately. For instance the fact that mathematical physics is so much more complex than sociology is a current situation, brought, on no doubt, by a badly skewed rate of development.

A clear statement of a problem, someone has said, is a necessary stage on the way to its solution. Let us assume that this generalization applies in the present instance, for it offers the only hope that we have to go on, and no one can live without hope.

Nevertheless the evidence of archaeology is clear: in geological time-frames, all animals eventually become extinct. That this must some day be the fate of the human species seems inevitable. Meanwhile, however, its living representatives march on their way, kicking and screaming while eating and killing everything in their way. Measured against the size and age of the cosmos, human life appears to be on such a small scale that its differences from other animals count for very little.

So long as the amount of false knowledge greatly exceeds the amount of known truth, we shall have to deal with the absolute believer. There is the difficulty that no way is known at present to apply the scientific method as developed by the physical sciences to the social area, but there is a way to imitate the virtue by following a few guide lines.

First off, be suspicious of any absolute formulation. (The scientist is not an absolute believer, only an interested investigator, with only hypotheses to match with the data). Regard no statement about the social subject matter as final. Try every approach to a problem that seems promising. Look to combine mathematical formulations with observations. Endeavor to disprove a plausible theory as a way of testing its validity. Remember that you are weaving a new cloth, not following an old thread.

Perhaps these guide lines undertaken as rules of procedure will help, but there are no guarantees. Nothing in the known history of the human species indicates that a social order can be put in place with any assurance that it will be permanent. The only permanent element is change, and so the old rules, whatever they were, are diminished as useful tools.

The nature of existence is that it is as much dynamic as static and contains as much energy as matter. Whether any government can prove strong enough to overcome all its rivals and establish a permanent global order remains to be seen. The only method for achieving such a condition, even temporarily, would have to lie through a balance of power. The only way a coalition could hope to escape the hegemony of its rivals would be to settle for compromise, however much it would have to surrender in this way and however uneasy such an arrangement might be.

Behind the concept of the balance of power, there must stand a consensus which reflects what all citizens everywhere earnestly want. Such a consensus could become the kind of global morality under which terrestrial man could live at peace with his fellows.

A compromise of this kind is not likely; but one is possible for it lies within the reach of present methods of education and cooperation. On the positive side of expediency, it seems the only short-range hope for the peaceful coexistence of men having fundamental differences of interest and outlook.

Meanwhile, the balance of power, though a basically unstable arrangement, has been infused with ultimate significance by the nature of advancing applied science and technology. The only known deterrent to the use of nuclear weapons by one side is the possession of those same weapons by the other, as is presently the case with the United States and the Soviet Union. The leaders of both countries recognize that neither has anything to gain from mutual destruction. Will this be true of Communist China in the future? Will it be true of those small nations who have the atomic bomb but over whose destinies less practical considerations may prevail; for instance, among leaders whose hold on positions of political power may be more tenuous?

The argument often made now, that with the discovery of thermonuclear bombs and global delivery systems weapons are so powerful that they are practically useless for any conventional aims, does not reckon with the natural ferocity of man. Those who insist that self-preservation is "the first law of nature" may be wrong, for more often than not hatred and enmity seem to take precedence. If men loved themselves more than they hated their enemies, they would not be willing to give their lives in war. There is more self-sacrifice involved in killing than there is in living. Evidently, a man is more willing to lay down his life that his fellows may die than that they may live.

The fact (if it is a fact) that no nation could win a thermonuclear war is insufficient to justify the prediction that none will wage it. Not everything nations do is in their own interest. The humanitarian pleas

that it would be inhuman to employ nuclear weapons comes only from those who
did not miss the tradition of humanism, but they are in the paralyzing
position of having been in the same generation responsible for both the
humanist tradition and the air raid. Poison gas was rarely used in recent
wars not because it was inhuman but because it was not practical. But,
according to The New York Times of July 21, 1967, the International Red
Cross again confirmed the story that Egyptian planes had been dropping posion
gas on Yemeni villages and the Russians are doing the same to the Afghans in
1984. Any effective weapon which seems to offer an advantage is sure to be
employed when the occasion arises.

It would be difficult for anyone who knows about the dark side of human
nature, its cruelty and its violence, not to hope for a favorable mutation
of the species. The best that we can want is the evolution of a more
admirable animal than the human. For the human species as now constituted
contains too much aggression in its intra-specific relations, too much
ferocity inherent in its very nature, to dream the dream of the ameliorative
liberals that man will come to live in accordance with his reason and
express only his essential goodness. Wars are inevitable so long as man
has his old ambition to dominate his environment by himself and, failing
that, collectively through the state.

It would not be difficult to show that political programs have an
adverse genetic effect. By killing off the healthiest and most able of the
young men who carry the best combination of genes, a nation can lose its
leadership and subside into the position of a second-class power.

But now the tables are turned and genetic programs are going to have
political effects. If molecular biologists can discover how to design the
kind of human beings it would be best to have, then of course everything in

human life, including social and political organizations, will be drastically affected. Let us hope there will be no parallel with the discoveries of the physicists, for it is the politicians who now have their fingers on the switch, and if those same politicans were to be put in possession of the discoveries of molecular biology, the results might be even worse.

There is still another possibility. A nuclear war might result in a mutation favorable to the species. This could be an unintended result but a happy one all the same. Animals undergo mutations when the necessity arises of adapting to a new environment. The artificial environment man has constructed out of the industrial culture of applied science and technology is new. We have noted already that almost nothing in his immediate surroundings, not even the earth he walks on or the air he breathes, is as it was before. He has altered all of it; either deliberately, as with cultivated and tilled soil or paved streets, or inadvertently, as with the polluted air of the cities. From man's effort to adapt to this new environment a mutation in his species can be expected, although certainly not soon. The process takes thousands of years; but if the industrial culture survives that long, it will provide the requisite selection pressures.

The adaptation to an artificial environment involves the exercise of the power of self-determination. The next step in the mutation cycle will occur when man is aware that he has this power, for then he can plan its use.

Let us say for instance that he wants to abolish war. The problem then has two approaches: first, that of genetic control, or the kind of inheritance it will be necessary to build into the human individual to reenforce his fellow feeling; second, that of environmental control, or the kind it is necessary to build for the human individual in order that he may adapt to it and so become more pacific. At the moment we do not have the answer to either question. But there is hope in both directions.

War and peace are not mere superficial opposites, they are opposites in detail. War cancels the meaning of everything achieved in peace as well as the peace itself. We know from experience that the best people as well as the worst will be destroyed; that the achievements of the fine arts and the experimental sciences, everything contained in the structures we have so painstakingly erected, from office buildings to cyclotrons and libraries, will perish in wars. Are we powerless to prevent them? Some doubt about that must always remain.

Thus our time in history is more significant than any other if only for one reason. We have reached the end of the road. The new weapons of destruction, and particularly the nuclear inter-continental missle, makes the rhythm of war and peace impossible. We are facing the choice of giving up war as part of a long-range social rhythm of war-and-peace or of accepting the total annihilation of the human species. It would not be the first one to become extinct but for the first time the choice is in human hands. What the outcome will be it is difficult at this stage to say. Perhaps momentous events will be the first to inform us, if there are any of us left to inform.

Notes

1 J. Q. Wilson and R. J. Herrnstein, Crime and Human Nature (New York 1985, Simon & Schuster), p. 22.
2 Gandhi, Autobiography, p. 241; Lorenz, On Aggression, p. 297.
3 C. J. Lumsden and E. O. Wilson, Translation of Epigenetic rules of individual behavior into ethnographic patterns (Proceedings of the National Academy of Sciences, U.S.A., 77:4382-86, 1980). Also by the same two authors, Genes, Mind and Culture (Cambridge, Mass., 1981, Harvard University Press).
4 R. C. Dutt, England and India (1785-1885, quoted in T. O. Lord, The British Empire 158-1983 (Oxford 1984, Oxford University Press), p. 148.

Chapter 15

POSSIBLE REMEDIES

1. Organic Extinctions

Coming to the end of this broad survey of destruction has brought us no closer to the prospect of "peace on earth, good will to all of mankind". Indeed the opposite is true: as the reader of any current newspaper or the watcher of any television news report can tell you, on all sides and over the entire globe, the aggression continues between individuals, between social groups, between nations, between blocs of states, until it seems almost as though the more two organizations of peoples have in common the more the single issue that sets them apart calls for violent confrontations.

Locally, crime is widely on the increase; murder, armed robbery, rape and arson are quite common. In the international picture, terrorism has become an increasing threat as well as an actuality, and one encouraged and prepared by national efforts, notably those of Syria, Libya and Iran. There are few quarters of the globe where there are no wars in progress, if we count the Soviets in Afghanistan, the Libyans in the Chad, the Iraquis and the Iranians on the Persian Gulf. The Lebanon calls for special mention, for not only do rival Moslem sects battle each other there but also conducted a running war with the Christian Lebanese, and all this independent of the kidnappings of many foreign nationals. Add to these the struggle between Protestant and Catholic in northern Ireland, between Fleming and Walloun in Belgium and hovering in the background always is the threat of a total nuclear war between the communist bloc of nations led by the Soviet Union and the western bloc led by the United States.

Indeed the case is worse than that. Given the prevalence of wars and other forms of aggression, it would seem that the human species devoting as it does at least half of all its energies to self-destruction, is bent on achieving its own extinction. Counting in all of the lethal activities it directs at other members, how can any hope to survive and continue the species?

The human species may be the only one bent on its own destruction, but in other cases nature takes a hand. From the account of the life-cycle of many organisms, it would appear that all must eventually become extinct. With regard to the process of killing, man is a mere amateur. There is no killer equal to nature, which has been responsible for the mass extinction of so many organic species. The list is impressive:

In the Cambrian era, some 600 million years ago, some 52 percent of all animal families became extinct, including the trilobites.

In the Devonian some 400 million years ago, many fish and sea creatures, including another 30 percent of all animal families, disappeared.

In the Permian, some 290 million years ago, half of all remaining animal families, especially the reptiles and most marine species, were lost.

In the Triassic, about 180 million years ago, some 400 genera of ammonoids, the molluscs, and a third of all animal families perished.

In the Cretaceous, 130 million years ago, the giant reptiles disappeared and at about 65 million years the dinosaurs joined them.

Finally, in the Pleistocene, one million years ago, most giant mammals, including mammoths, mastodons and ground sloths died out.

The human species has one thing going for it that the others do not. It has reproduced itself exponentially until literally it covers most of the habitable land and even some that seems uninhabitable. The earliest bands of humans were small, numbering at most a few hundred. They reproduced themselves so rapidly, once they mastered the trick of settled civilizations with animal husbandry and agriculture, that they now number in the billions; and from their original homes in Africa and Asia they have spread all over the globe until they have produced a situation which if allowed to continue will result in standing room only.

However, the threat of nuclear war cancels all the advantage that immense numbers provided, for it has been argued that there is no safe refuge, no hiding place, that the radiation cannot reach. Thus on any grounds the human species is not only an endangered species -- in these terms they all are -- but a doomed species as well.

Of course that is not the whole story. If the human species does not finally succeed in ending its own existence, nature can be counted on to do it. If all organic species eventually become extinct, then unless some presently unforeseen circumstance arises we can expect the same fate for the human. Life does not exist in a vacuum, but hitherto the part played by non-human nature has been neglected. That, as we shall presently see, is no longer possible.

It is time, then, to go global, to view in a cosmic setting some of the problems and suggested solutions we have been considering. We are all riding on the same planet and must translate our predicament into astronomical terms. The relation of the species to its environment must now for the first time take into account the _extent_ of that environment. There is a great deal of very recently acquired information which might have some bearing on how we can expect human behavior to be received in the future, information not just about man in society nor about man on the continents or even about man on earth but about man in the universe. That is paradoxically the only place no one has looked. I propose to look at it now.

2. The Cosmic Prospect

Within the last century, and especially in the last few decades, the flow of new information about the astronomical universe and its contents has been expanded greatly. New theories of how the cosmos was formed and what it contains were introduced. New instruments of observation as well as new techniques and locations for them have greatly increased the sum of knowledge.   We know now, in short, a lot more than we knew before.

The universe is evidently far larger than we had supposed. Measured in light-years or the distance light can travel in a vacuum in one year, which is equal to 9.4605 million kilometers, our galaxy, the Milky Way, is estimated to be about 100,000 light-years in diameter and to contain some 300 billion stars; and there are known to be millions of such galaxies. Our sun is of course a star, and takes 250 million years to complete an orbit around the center of the Milky Way.

Stars are formed from collapsing clouds of gas. They continue to exist by burning as fuel the hydrogen in their interiors. When the star first condenses it is very red and intensely luminous but as it contracts it exhausts its supply of nuclear fuel, and when it can no longer contain its own gravitational force it first expands and then explodes, and the outer layer is blown off. Such a supernova explosion signals that a star has died.

Our sun is such a star; it has existed for some 4.5 billion years and has an equal amount of time left, and when toward the end of its cycle it expands, it will include the planets and destroy them.

In a word, nothing last forever, not stars, not even galaxies; ultimate destruction is the fate of all. Even if there is life on other planets circling other suns in other galaxies, all such members of the human species will still have a limited life-cycle. For everything in the astronomical universe is marked for extinction. What is involved, then, is only a difference in time-spans. Generally speaking, the larger the unit the longer the survival: suns survive longer than planets, galaxies longer than suns; but the end of all is the same.

One of the central facts of the astronomical universe is called entropy, the tendency of all disorder to increase. According to the second law of thermodynamics in statistical mechanics, disorganization is the rule. The single exception to this seems to be organic evolution, in which the tendency to order increases. The only question is, how long can this reversal of the general rule continue? Looking back at the progress of organic evolution, it seems to have gone from the monkeys to the humanoids, and finally to the human species.

That is not the only reversal, there are others; but they become lost in the general picture, which always works only one way. The Andromeda galaxy seems to be drifting in our direction, a tendency opposed to the Hubble expansion of space, which has been justified conclusively in its finding that all galaxies and indeed all astronomical bodies are drifting apart. So the question remains: how long and to what extent can any exception

prevail in its own narrow domain? We know that nature, then, is the
ultimate killer, and despite temporary setbacks will see the destroyers
destroyed. The cosmic drawn has only one ending.

3. Possible Alternatives

Anyone who has seen the photographs of the earth taken from the moon
by the astronauts is sure to be made keenly aware of the predicament of the
human species, isolated as it is on the surface of a minor planet orbiting
the sun, and held there only through the pull of gravitation. There is
every reason to seek survival if it can be managed by the whole species
working together as a unit and abandoning whatever differences and frictions
exist that might set its members apart.

Given that there is in fact no exception to the eventual destruction of
everything in the cosmos, even if the extinction of the human species
cannot be avoided it can be postponed. I can think of four ways that this
can be accomplished, though no doubt there are others: (1) the rule of law
can be made global; (2) colonies can be established on other planets where
the same inevitability of extinction does not necessarily apply; (3) the
human species can mutate to other forms more likely to survive by changing
the immediate environment to which the human species must adapt; and,
finally, (4) the mutation of the species by genetics can be favorably
controlled.

(1) The rule of law, that is, agreements backed by force, is at present
limited to nation-states. International laws are mere agreements which are
often broken without penalty: there is no international rule of law which
is backed by force. Wars of course automatically cancel all international

agreements.

The only hope for a permanent world peace is the establishment of a global rule of law with penalties for infraction. This could presumably be accomplished if all nations wanted it, for each could contribute a portion of the total militia which could be devoted to preventing or punishing infractions. That would require a world population intent on bringing about and preserving such a situation, which under current circumstances seems unlikely. It is, however, a goal to work toward, with the understanding that nothing less will insure survival.

There is a hint in the behavior of citizens in war time. Faced with a common enemy, people tend to sink their differences and to band together for greater effectiveness. For example in world war 2, priests and communists joined criminals and others in addition to democrats to fight their common enemy, the Nazis. Whatever is to be done to save the human species its members must do together, and even if the case is almost hopeless it is still the thing to do.

It can have one effective if temporary outcome: the elimination of all lesser conflicts. The rule of law, which has worked successfully in the democracies as well as in some monarchies, in ancient Rome for instance, as well as in modern western Europe and the United States. Establishing it globally might at the very least compel all peoples to face together what is a common problem. A global rule of law would give to all of humanity the power of a concerted effort, and who knows what that could accomplish?

(2) If life on earth is doomed to extinction, what about the possibilities elsewhere? Can the human species spread the risk by moving to other planets within the solar system? The possibilities need to be explored.

The Soviets already have an orbiting space station and plan others. NASA has similar ventures on the drawing board. In these and other ways perhaps the limitations of an earth-bound existence can be avoided, not by any permanent establishment of life, since nothing in the universe lasts forever, but perhaps by extending it somewhat.

Given the known forms of energy, the prospect of getting outside the solar system and perhaps even the Milky Way seems remote. But then we must remember that many accomplishments made familiar to us in the last half century seemed utterly impossible not too long ago. Who a hundred years ago could have dreamed of putting a man on the moon and getting him back again, or of having a flourishing international air travel of the kind that spans the oceans every one of the 24 hours these days? What is commonplace now was unthinkable only a few decades back. Who knows, then, what the possibilities in the future are? There may be other forms of energy besides the ones we now recognize, and faster forms of locomotion that might by some previously undiscovered technology exceed the speed of light. Thus the prospect of moving to other planets, to other solar systems, even to other galaxies, should not be dismissed out of hand even though, it is impossible now.

The human species is quite young, only some 40,000 years old, making it the youngest of the organic species. Its accomplishments are even more recent, as we have just seen much less than a century old. The remarkable achievements in both knowledge and accomplishments in so short a time open up the not impossible prospect of even greater ones in the future. Extinction for a species can come at any moment -- there are so many possibilities of danger -- but on the other hand it can be put off for quite a while. If the cockroach and the horseshoe crab can last as species for millions of years, then given a favorable environment perhaps the human species can do so also. And in that time who knows what it can get done?

(3) Its recent accomplishments have all resulted from a single trick: learning to transform the immediate environment by turning portions of it against itself. From pure science to applied science and from applied science to technology, the road to greater control of human life lies outside that life in the world it occupies. Perhaps the greater road to the survival of the species by postponing its extinction lies along the same lines of advance. All of the experimental physical sciences have taught the members of the human species how to improve the environment. That is sure to have repercussions on the character of future generations. If the human organism is in any way responsive to its adaptation to a changing environment, then who knows what the future of the species will be? For the environment has changed radically, as anyone who bothers to journey from the center of a city to the unimproved countryside can readily see.

This development is a fairly new affair. The discovery of animal husbandry and agriculture are only some 10,000 years old, and already human life has been transformed by them. However, the principle involved has not as yet been cultivated on its own. If the members of the human species were to decide what sort of animal they wanted to be, presumably some sort superior to what prevails now, and then work out the kind of environment, artificial or no, that would by adaptation produce it, they could no doubt be successful. That is the next task confronting a species that would survive and escape extinction or at least postpone it indefinitely.

(4) The final way to postpone the extinction of the human species might lie in the possibility of controlling mutation. Modern man is the result of a chain of accidental mutations. The chimpanzee, our closest

relation, and ourselves had a common ancestor only 4½ million years ago.
It all goes back to the molecule of deoxyribonucleic acid, "DNA". The DNA
chains of human, chimpanzee and gorilla are identical along 98 percent of
their lengths. The remaining 2 percent accounts for all of the unique
features of humanity.[1]

If so much was the result of chance, what might not be done with careful
planning? There are already excellent examples of the possibilities in the
work of the geneticists with plants and animals. Much improved species of
wheat and cattle testify to the success of experiments conducted in many of
the agricultural colleges in our state universities. Thus far, many
responsible individuals and authorities shrink with horror at the prospect of
tampering with the human gene. The Nazis gave such work a very bad name. But
there are other, more favorable prospects, and if the very survival of the
human species depended on them, it might mean viewing them in a more hopeful
way.

For example, a more pacific human nature might be cultivated and the human
species in that guise less bent on self-destruction. If it did not survive,
at least the fault would lie elsewhere and the suicidal tendency on which it
seems currently bent might be avoided. A firm line would be necessary to
eliminate the ferocious aggression which accounts for wars and yet keep
sufficient power to provide for the construction on which civilization
depends. Genetic engineering has not yet reached that stage of competence,
but iwth more time and study it might; and if it were known that all the
hope of survival lies in that direction, the efforts could be doubled.

Notes

1 There are many accounts of DNA. One of the best, and the one I have
relied on the most is John Gribbin, In Search of The Double Helix
(London 1985, Wilwood House Ltd.). See especially p. 342 ff.

INDEX

INDEX

INDEX

INDEX

INDEX

Heyerdahl, T., 25
High civilizations, warlike, 53
Hijacking, 101
Hindu vs. Moslem, slaughters by, 91
Hitler, A., and Stalin, 139; and torture, 105
Hitler's Germany, 74
Hittites, 85
Hobbes, T., 31
Hogg, Gary, 21
Holocaust of Hitler, 90
Homer, 53
Homo faber, 14
Human as omnivore, 12
Human body, 40% muscle, 11
Human destiny, uncontrolled, 40
Human environment, artificial, 14
Human extinction, inevitable, 160
Human life, reason for, 74
Human nature, 49; as aggressive, 6
Human reproduction unchecked, 169
Human self-destruction, 168
Human species doomed, 169
Humanism, 49; in reverse, 130; tradition of, 92
Humanist revolution in Europe, 147
Humanity, common guilt of, 94
Huns, 87
Hunter, as killer, 9
Hunter-gatherers, 10
Hunting, as sport, 51; as way of life, 10f.
Hunting as torture, 108
Hydrogen bomb, 39

Ideal of social laws, 156
Ideal society, 154, 158
Ideologies, 61
Idi Amin of Uganda, 27
Ignorance, nature of, 61
Ik, people of the, 100
Indian independence, 91
Information, need for, 107
Intercontinental ballistic missles, 39
"Internal exile", 132
International law, 42
International terrorists, 122
Intra-specific aggression, 55
Irrationality of reason, 50
Isocrates, 98, 104

INDEX

INDEX

INDEX

INDEX

INDEX

INDEX

John D. Rosecrance

THE DEGENERATES OF LAKE TAHOE
A Study of Persistence in the Social World of Horse Race Gambling

American University Studies: Series XI (Anthropology and Sociology).
Vol. 8
ISBN 0-8204-0187-0   181 pages   hardcover US $ 23.15*

*Recommended price - alterations reserved

Horse racing is America's number one spectator sport. It is also an important social phenomenon affecting the daily lives of millions of people. The behaviour patterns of inveterate horse players are here, for the first time, thoroughly investigated.

The author, who is himself a veteran horse player, has selected 65 fellow gamblers for his study. He identifies and analyses the social-psychological components involved in sustained participation at gambling. He addresses the perplexing question of why gamblers persist at an activity that is so personally costly.

This book provides valuable insight into the phenomenom of sustained gambling and since several state legislatures are considering bills to legalize off-track betting, both advocates and opponents of such legislation would appreciate the scientifically developed information concerning already established off-track betting groups.

Contents: The social world of the inveterate horse race gambler is analysed from an insider's perspective. The researcher identifies and describes the social-psychological components involved in sustained participation at gambling

PETER LANG PUBLISHING, INC.
62 West 45th Street
USA – New York, NY 10036